TREASURE

UNCOVERING PRINCIPLES THAT GOVERN SUCCESS

Ed Cole

The Most Widely-Read Men's Author in the World

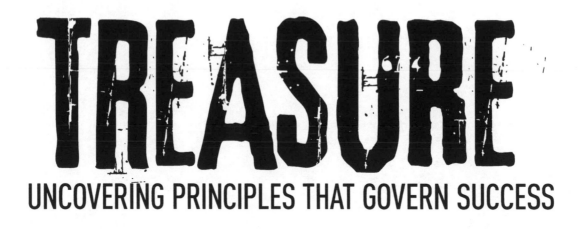

TREASURE

UNCOVERING PRINCIPLES THAT GOVERN SUCCESS

WHITAKER
HOUSE

TREASURE WORKBOOK:
Uncovering Principles That Govern Success

Christian Men's Network
P.O. Box 3
Grapevine, TX 76099
ChristianMensNetwork.com
Email: office@ChristianMensNetwork.com

Facebook.com/EdwinLouisCole

ISBN: 979-8-88769-149-7
Printed in the United States of America
© 2020 by Edwin and Nancy Cole Legacy LLC

Published by:
Whitaker House
1030 Hunt Valley Circle
New Kensington, PA 15068

Majoring in Men® and Resolute Books™ is a registered trademark of Edwin and Nancy Cole Legacy LLC.

CONTENTS

LESSON 1
THE BASIS FOR A GREAT LIFE

LESSON 1

THE BASIS FOR A GREAT LIFE

A. Every thing in life is _____. *(page 9)*

B. Living on principles is: *(circle one) (page 9)*

    entertaining   boring   life changing

C. Principles are what four things: *(page 9)*

    Basic _____

    Fundamental _____

    Facts _____

    Primary _____

  1. Give an example of a principle of the universe. *(pages 9–10)*

    _____

  2. Discovering principles is a lifelong passion for successful people. *(page 10)*

    ____ True   ____ False

FOR FURTHER STUDY

God's Word gives patterns and principles to overcome any obstacle, enemy, or attack: *"Is not my word like as a fire? saith the Lord; and like a hammer that breaketh the rock in pieces?"* (Jeremiah 23:29); *"For with God nothing is ever impossible and no word from God shall be without power or impossible of fulfillment"* (Luke 1:37 AMPC).

Godly principles are relevant (see Numbers 23:19; Deuteronomy 29:29.): *"This book of the law shall not depart out of thy mouth; but thou shalt meditate therein day and night, that thou mayest observe to do according to all that is written therein: for then thou shalt make thy way prosperous, and then thou shalt have good success"* (Joshua 1:8; see also Psalm 9:7–10; 90:1–2; Jeremiah 31:33; Malachi 3:6-7; Hebrews 8:10; James 1:17. Determine to follow after success and godliness (see Deuteronomy 8:18): *"I will speak of thy testimonies also before kings, and will not be ashamed. …O how love I thy law! It is my meditation all the day"* (Psalm 119:46, 97; see also Romans 1:16.)

3. People who live by _____, _____, or _____ lack bedrock on which to build their lives. *(page 10)*

How do they usually end up and why? *(page 10)*

_____

_____

4. People who make decisions by personality or preference can be talked out of their decisions from one day to the next. *(page 10)*

____ True   ____ False

5. The more you build your life on principle, the higher your _____, the straighter your _____, and the greater your _____. *(page 10)*

D.   Patterns are ways in which the universe operates. Give some examples. *(page 10)*

_____

_____

_____

_____

1. Discovering and uncovering workable patterns is an aim of successful management, corporations and individuals. *(page 11)*

____ True   ____ False

2.   The pattern you learn determines the _____ you _____.

The _____ the pattern, the better the _____. *(page 11)*

_____

FOR FURTHER STUDY

The more we base our lives on principles, the straighter our course will be: *"the good and the right way"* (1 Samuel 12:23); *"Thou has enlarged my steps under me; so that my feet did not slip"* (2 Samuel 22:37; see also Psalm 5:8; Proverbs 3:23; 4:11–12).

Everything God does is according to a pattern, based on a principle: *"See, saith he, that thou make all things according to the pattern shown to thee in the mount"* (Hebrews 8:5). *"May God's mercy and peace be upon all of you who live by this principle and upon those everywhere who are really God's own"* (Galatians 6:16 TLB; see also Exodus 25:8–9; 1 Chronicles 28:11).

All principles of human society are basically kingdom principles. (See Romans 11:36; 1 Corinthians 8:6; Colossians 1:16-17.)

It is God's desire for His church to know His patterns and principles: *"The secret things belong unto the LORD our God: but those things which are revealed belong unto us and to our children for ever, that we may do all the words of this law"* (Deuteronomy 29:29).

E. _____ are your best friend. *(page 11)*

    1. List five benefits of reading: *(page 11)*

        Develops the power of _____

        Develops the power of _____ _____

        Provides greater _____

        Provides sharpness of _____

        Provides enjoyment of _____

    2. The loss of the habit of reading is a gain in the realm of _____. *(page 12)*

    3. Reading is the most inexpensive thing a parent can do with a family—not reading is the most expensive. *(page 12)*

        _____ True   _____ False

    4. *In your own words*, explain why books are weapons against the cultural malaise of our day. *(pages 12–13)*

    _____

    _____

    _____

    _____

    5. How is truth like soap? *(page 13)*

    _____

    _____

FOR FURTHER STUDY:

Practice: the highest learning level: *"So everyone who hears these words of Mine and acts upon them [obeying them] will be like a sensible (prudent, practical, wise) man who built his house upon the rock"* (Matthew 7:24 AMPC); *"Wisdom gives: a long, good life, riches, honor, pleasure, peace"* (Proverbs 3:16–17 TLB); *"For the Lord grants wisdom! His every word is a treasure of knowledge and understanding"* (Proverbs 2:6 TLB; see also Proverbs 4:7; 8:11).

Understanding is applied, anointed common sense. (See Proverbs 2:7–8, 4:5.)

Truth is not an option in life: *"Speak ye every man the truth to his neighbour; execute the judgment of truth and peace in your gates"* (Zechariah 8:16); It is the bedrock of integrity. (See Psalm 24:4–5.) *"Through thy precepts I get understanding: therefore I hate every false way"* (Psalm 119:104); *"And ye shall know the truth, and the truth shall make you free"* (John 8:32).

F.   Business is not about money or toys but: *(circle one)* *(page 13)*

> How well you outsmart the competition.
>
> Getting by with as little effort as possible to earn a paycheck.
>
> The level of life on which you want to live.

1. Promotions always turn out to be positive changes. *(pages 13–15)*

_____ True   _____ False

2. What is an inescapable lifelong pattern for successful people? *(page 16)*

Passing through the stages of _____ that take us to new _____, some which require starting at the _____.

G.   Once you make a choice, you become the _____ to that choice. *(circle one)* *(page 16)*

coach   master   servant   director   observer

H.   Write the correct letter in the blank that completes the sentences. *(page 17)*

_____ Decision translates into   a. productivity

_____ Energy enables a man to achieve his   b. energy

_____ Choosing not to decide becomes   c. choice

_____ Man must exercise his power over   d. goals

_____ Indecision saps   e. a decision in itself

FOR FURTHER STUDY

Indecisiveness: *"A double minded man is unstable in all his ways"* (James 1:8).

The double-minded waiver between right and wrong because they are undecided: *"Elijah…said, How long halt ye between two opinions?"* (1 Kings 18:21).

They profess to hate sin but have a lingering love for it: *"What is causing the quarrels and fights among you? Isn't it because there is a whole army of evil desires within you?"* (James 4:1 TLB). They do not have a right understanding of good and evil: *"But solid food is for the mature, who by constant use have trained themselves to distinguish good from evil"* (Hebrews 5:14 NIV); *"I have refrained my feet from every evil way, that I might keep thy word. I have not departed from thy judgments: for thou hast taught me"* (Psalm 119:101–102).

Decision translates into energy, which motivates to action: *"And Solomon determined to build an house for the name of the Lord"* (2 Chronicles 2:1).

I. Check True or False for the following sentences: *(pages 17–19)*

Circumstances determine your level of life. _____ True _____ False

Choices have consequences. _____ True _____ False

You can change your life by changing your choices. _____ True _____ False

Today's choice is insurance against tomorrow. _____ True _____ False

Life just happens, so a man has no choice but to react. _____ True _____ False

J. Choices determine what three things? *(page 18)*

_____   _____   _____

K. Claiming victim status… *(complete the sentences) (page 18–19)*

…excuses people from _____ for their own _____

and creates frivolous _____.

L. Refusing to exercise your power of choice allows others to _____ it for you.

Allowing others to make your choices for you allows them to _____

your _____, and when they do, they _____ make it too

_____. *(page 19)*

FOR FURTHER STUDY

The principles upon which to build your life: *"Get wisdom, get understanding: forget it not; neither decline from the words of my mouth. Forsake her not, and she shall preserve thee: love her and she shall keep thee. Wisdom is the principal thing; therefore get wisdom: and with all thy getting get understanding"* (Proverbs 4:5–8; see also Psalm 119:133; James 1:5, 3:13–17).

Choices: *"I have set before you life and death, blessing and cursing: therefore choose life, that both thou and thy seed may live"* (Deuteronomy 30:19).

The freedom to choose between alternatives is the only true freedom in life. (See Galatians 5:13.) We can choose to succeed or to fail; we can be wise or ignorant. (See Psalm 90:12.) Don't waste your youth brooding over what someone else has done to you. (See Isaiah 43:14, 18.)

Make changes: *"When I became a man, I put away childish things"* (1 Corinthians 13:11).

Be renewed: *"Put off…the old man…be renewed in the spirit of your mind;…put on the new man, which after God is created in righteousness and true holiness"* (Ephesians 4:22–24).

M. Write the correct letter in the blank that completes the sentences. *(pages 19–21)*

_____ Life is composed of your choices and a. constructed by your words.

_____ Once you choose to build a new life b. are two of your best tools.

_____ You are only committed to c. creative power.

_____ Every word you speak has d. change your words.

_____ Use your words wisely e. and you will prosper.

_____ Your choices and words f. what you confess.

N. Change is... *(page 21)*

_____ , _____ , and _____ .

1. To change from one level to the next requires three actions: *(page 22)*

Stepping out of a _____ _____

Dying to an _____ _____

Breaking away from a _____ way of _____

2. The man who knows *how* will always have a _____ ; the man who knows *why* will always be his _____ . *(page 22)*

3. Master the _____ by which something works, or the _____ on which it rests, and you'll rise above your peers. *(page 22)*

FOR FURTHER STUDY

Words have power (see Psalm 15:1–4; 119:130): *"Evil words destroy; godly skill rebuilds"* (Proverbs 11:9 TLB; see also Proverbs 12:6); *"Words of the wise soothe and heal"* Proverbs 12:18 TLB); *"A word of encouragement does wonders!"* (Proverbs 12:25 TLB); *"He that keepeth his mouth keepeth his life; but he that openeth wide his lips shall have destruction"* (Proverbs 13:3); *"Gentle words cause life and health; griping brings discouragement"* (Proverbs 15:4 TLB); *"Death and life are in the power of the tongue"* (Proverbs 18:21; see also Romans 16:18).

We must watch our word (see Proverbs 6:2; Colossians 4:6; James 3:2, 9–10): *"Keep control of your tongue, and guard your lips from telling lies"* (1 Peter 3:10 TLB).

God holds us accountable for our words: *"Every idle word that men shall speak, they shall give account thereof in the day of judgment"* (Matthew 12:36).

As long as a man's words live, he lives: *"There is living truth in what a good man says"* (Proverbs 10:11 TLB).

O.   Be willing to _____. *(complete these sentences)* *(pages 22–23)*

1. _____ are like keys to unlock doors formerly closed to you.

2. Patterns are like maps to guide you from _____ _____ to the _____.

3. Learning life's patterns and principles is a _____ _____.

4. _____ is more important than availability.

5. Learning requires a _____ for _____ and a desire to be _____.

6. _____ is the core of ignorance, because an ignorant person is too _____ to _____.

7. Shun _____!

8. _____.

9. Learn the _____.

10. Master the _____.

11. Have the _____ to _____.

FOR FURTHER STUDY

Wisdom: The fear of the Lord is *"the beginning of knowledge: but fools despise wisdom and instruction"* (Proverbs 1:7); *"to hate evil: pride, and arrogancy, and the evil way, and the froward mouth, do I hate"* (Proverbs 8:13); *"the beginning of wisdom: and the knowledge of the holy is understanding"* (Proverbs 9:10).

Make changes: *"Plant the good seeds of righteousness and you will reap a crop of my love; plow the hard ground of your hearts, for now is the time to seek the Lord, that he may come and shower salvation upon you"* (Hosea 10:12 TLB); *"If you are angry, don't sin by nursing your grudge. Don't let the sun go down with you still angry—get over it quickly; for when you are angry you give a mighty foothold to the devil"* (Ephesians 4:26–27 TLB; see also Hebrews 3:7–8).

Change begins with you: *"Each of us must bear some faults and burdens of his own. For none of us is perfect!"* (Galatians 6:5 TLB).

The mature person is willing to admit he is wrong and to change: *"Asa…took courage…put away the abominable idols…renewed the altar of the Lord"* (2 Chronicles 15:8; see also Proverbs 28:13).

PRACTICAL:

1. What may be going on when middle-age men and women mentally return to their "glory days"? What is the "remedy"?

_____

_____

_____

2. "You are only committed to what you confess." Explain what this means.

_____

_____

_____

Do you need to change your confession about anything? *(not necessary to write out)*

REPEAT THIS PRAYER OUT LOUD:

Father, please help me discover Your principles and establish positive patterns to live the great life You desire for me. I pray the choices I make and the words I speak will be wise and productive. Forgive my stubbornness. I choose to learn, to read and to have the courage to change. In Jesus's name, I pray. Amen.

FOR FURTHER STUDY

The core of ignorance is stubbornness: *"My people are destroyed for lack of knowledge: because thou hast rejected knowledge"* (Hosea 4:6). Men repeat mistakes because they never learn from them, never learned how to learn (see Proverbs 9:7–9; 10:8): *"As a dog returneth to his vomit, so a fool returneth to his folly"* (Proverbs 26:11); *"Let the godly smite me! It will be a kindness! If they reprove me, it is medicine! Don't let me refuse it. But I am in constant prayer against the wicked and their deeds"* (Psalm 141:5 TLB).

Pattern for Increase	Pattern for Failure
Identification (Acts 2:42–43)	Deception (Genesis 3:4–5)
Involvement (Acts 2:44)	Distraction (Genesis 3:6)
Investment (Acts 2:45)	Dislocation (Genesis 3:7–10)
Increase (Acts 2:46–47)	Destruction (Genesis 3:23)

SELF-TEST—LESSON 1

1. _____ are people's best friends.

2. The loss of the habit of reading is a gain in the realm of _____.

3. Discovering principles is a lifelong passion for successful people.

    _____ True   _____ False

4. Once you make a choice, you become the _____ to that choice.

5. Choices have consequences.

    _____ True   _____ False

6. Life is composed of your choices and constructed by your words.

    _____ True   _____ False

7. Decision translates into _____, which enables us to achieve our _____.

8. Choices determine what three things:

    _____, _____ , and _____

9. You are only committed to what you confess.

    _____ True   _____ False

10. Every word you speak has _____ _____.

11. Teachability is more important than availability.

    _____ True   _____ False

12. Learning requires a heart for _____ and a desire to be _____.

LESSON 2
DREAM YOUR FUTURE, THEN DO IT

DREAM YOUR FUTURE, THEN DO IT

A. The most powerful thing you can do in life is: *(circle one)* *(page 27)*

own a business   create an image   run for office   win the lottery

1. Images compel and propel us. *(page 27)*

_____ True _____ False

2. Images in our minds drive us toward our _____. *(page 27)*

B. _____ are the _____ of every great _____ in life.

(use words from the following list) *(page 27)*

filters   achievement   dreams   sports   promotion   substance

1. People's dreams of achievement are the basis for what they do—or don't do—in life. *(page 27)*

_____ True _____ False

2. Most people dream too small. *(page 28)*

_____ True _____ False

FOR FURTHER STUDY

Images have a powerful influence on our lives: *"As he thinketh in his heart, so is he"* (Proverbs 23:7; see also Titus 1:15).

Create an image: *"Their idols are silver and gold, the work of men's hands. ...They that make them are like unto them; so is every one that trusteth in them"* (Psalm 115:4, 8).

Destroy an image. (See Numbers 33:52.)

Joseph's God-given dream established an image in his mind of who he was and who he was to become. (See Genesis 37:5–11.)

Become new in Christ: *"It doesn't make any difference now whether we have been circumcised or not; what counts is whether we really have been changed into new and different people"* (Galatians 6:15 TLB).

Images in our mind motivate our behavior: *"For out of the heart proceed evil thoughts, murders, adulteries, fornications, thefts, false witness, blasphemies"* (Matthew 15:19; see also Romans 1:22-25).

3. *In your own words*, explain the "woulda-coulda-shoulda" crowd. *(page 28)*

_____

_____

_____

4. The image in your mind determines your _____ because dreams _____ you toward your _____ like a _____. The more specific your _____, the more powerful the pull. *(page 28)*

5. Why is it important to recreate altered, stolen and destroyed dreams into a positive vision of your future? *(page 28)*

_____

6. A positive vision creates _____, a sense of _____ and _____. *(page 28)*

FOR FURTHER STUDY

God wants us to grow, to fulfill our dream: *"I commend you to God, and to the word of his grace, which is able to build you up, and to give you an inheritance among all them which are sanctified"* (Acts 20:32); *"But grow in grace, and in the knowledge of our Lord and Saviour Jesus Christ"* (2 Peter 3:18).

We can be seriously restricted by others' images of us: i.e., Joseph (see Genesis 37:19–20), David (see 1 Samuel 17:28–29), and Mary and Martha (see Luke 10:38–42).

Don't allow someone's unbelief, rejection of truth, or refusal to grow stop your dream: *"Caleb stilled the people before Moses and said…we are well able to overcome it"* (Numbers 13:30).

Our early experiences create images that have great influence (see 2 Timothy 1:5): *"From a child thou hast known the holy scriptures"* (2 Timothy 3:15).

Teach children to discern right from wrong: *"Train up a child in the way he should go: and when he is old, he will not depart from it"* (Proverbs 22:6).

C. A person without a vision is a person without a future. *(page 29)*

    ____ True   ____ False

D. A person without a future will always return to his past. *(page 29)*

    ____ True   ____ False

E. _____ the vision, because it doesn't become a _____ until you are _____ to what you _____. Seeing it in writing makes it seem _____. *(page 30)*

F. Dreaming without doing is _____. Doing what you dream is _____. You have to _____ your dream. *(page 31)*

1. What you _____ has the greatest _____ for _____ or _____ in your life because you are _____ to your _____. *(use words from the following list)* *(page 31)*

potential   beliefs   harm   believe   harnessed   good

2. Right believing has a _____ burden; wrong believing has a _____ burden. *(page 31)*

3. All wrong conduct is based on wrong believing. *(page 31)*

    ____ True   ____ False

FOR FURTHER STUDY

Write down what God taught you today and what He teaches you day by day in the future (see Deuteronomy 6:6, 9; 1 Timothy 4:14-16): *"Write the things which thou hast seen, and the things which are, and the things which shall be hereafter"* (Revelation 1:19).

Write down your decision, so you'll be motivated to hold to it: *"Write the vision, and make it plain upon tables, that he may run that readeth it"* (Habakkuk 2:2).

Goals require dedication (see Joshua 11:15–16): *"As the time approached for him to be taken up to heaven, Jesus resolutely set out for Jerusalem"* (Luke 9:51 NIV; see also 1 Timothy 1:18; 6:12); *"I have fought the good fight, I have finished the race, I have kept the faith"* (2 Timothy 4:7 NIV).

Choose wisely: *"Every prudent man deals with knowledge, but a [self-confident] fool exposes and flaunts his folly"* (Proverbs 13:16 AMPC); *"Buy the truth, and sell it not; also wisdom, and instruction, and understanding"* (Proverbs 23:23).

G. In the blanks, write the correct letter that completes the sentences. *(page 31–32)*

_____ To change your conduct,   a. look for opportunities.

_____ If you believe you're going to succeed,   b. you'll invest.

_____ If you believe you're going to be rich,   c. you'll pursue them.

_____ If you believe you can achieve your dreams,   d. change your beliefs.

_____ If you believe you're going to be thin,   e. you'll eat right.

H. *In your own words*, explain: "Perceptions create personal realities." *(page 32)*

_____

_____

I. The more our perceptions align with _____, the more _____ we can become because _____ sets us _____. *(page 32)*

J. What you think in your heart determines what you _____.

(circle one) (page 32)

have for lunch   do on vacation   become

1. What you believe will either _____ or _____. *(page 32)*

2. You are yoked to your beliefs. *(page 32)*

_____ True   _____ False

FOR FURTHER STUDY

Men repeat mistakes because they never learn from them, never learned how to learn (see Proverbs 9:7–9; 10:8): *"As a dog returneth to his vomit, so a fool returneth to his folly"* (Proverbs 26:11); *"Let the godly smite me! It will be a kindness! If they reprove me, it is medicine! Don't let me refuse it. But I am in constant prayer against the wicked and their deeds"* (Psalm 141:5 TLB).

Our images must be renewed (see 1 Samuel 17:32): *"Be not conformed to this world: but be ye transformed by the renewing of your mind"* (Romans 12:2); *"Be renewed in the spirit of your mind"* (Ephesians 4:22–23); *"But we all, with open face beholding as in a glass the glory of the Lord, are changed into the same image from glory to glory, even as by the Spirit of the Lord"* (2 Corinthians 3:18; see also John 5:44; 1 Corinthians 6:20; 2 Corinthians 5:17; 1 Peter 1:18–21).

Believe in your heart that God cares for you (see Psalm 139:13–14): *"Thoughts of peace…and not of evil, to give you an expected end"* (Jeremiah 29:11; see also Matthew 10:29–31).

Determine to live up to the potential God placed within you: *"I press on to take hold of that for which Christ Jesus took hold of me"* (Philippians 3:12 NIV).

K. Faith is believing that what you cannot see will _____ to _____. (*page 32*)

Fear is believing that what you cannot see will _____ to _____. (*page 32*)

Faith attracts the _____, while fear attracts the _____. (*page 32*)

Faith attracts _____, _____ and _____. In finances, when we put faith to work, faith attracts _____. (*page 33*)

Fear attracts _____, _____, and _____. (*page 33*)

1. People with faith _____ _____ before waiting for the _____ _____. (*page 33*)

2. Not everyone has a measure of faith. (*page 33*)

_____ True   _____ False

3. The evidence that we are using faith is in our _____. Faith is belief in _____. (*page 33*)

FOR FURTHER STUDY

Have faith: "*The righteous will live by faith*" (Galatians 3:11 NIV); "*Through faith we understand that the worlds were framed by the word of God, so that things which are seen were not made of things which do appear*" (Hebrews 11:3).

Financial health based on faith: "*What things soever ye desire, when ye pray, believe that ye receive them, and ye shall have them*" (Mark 11:24); "*It is your Father's good pleasure to give you the kingdom*" (Luke 12:32); "*He which soweth sparingly shall reap also sparingly; and he which soweth bountifully shall reap also bountifully*" (2 Corinthians 9:6; see also James 2:17–20).

What you believe can attract or repel (see Genesis 39:2–5): "*For the thing which I greatly feared is come upon me, and that which I was afraid of is come unto me*" (Job 3:25); "*It is possible to give away and become richer! It is also possible to hold on too tightly and lose everything. Yes, the liberal man shall be rich! By watering others, he waters himself. …Trust in your money and down you go! Trust in God and flourish as a tree!*" (Proverbs 11:24, 28 TLB; see also Mark 11:23).

L.   Your _____, based on what you believe, will make you your own best _____ or worst _____. (*page 35*)

     1. You will always rise to the level of your _____. (*page 35*)

     2. The way you live and the level you achieve is determined by: (*page 35*)

         a. the hidden _____ of your _____

M.   *In your own words*, explain this phrase: "To guard your vision, you must guard what you allow into your life." (*page 35*)

_____

_____

_____

_____

     1. Private philosophy determines public performance. (*page 36*)

         ____ True   ____ False

     2. The only principle you really believe is: (*circle one*) (*page 37*)

     what's underlined in your Bible   your dad's advice   the one you obey

     3. _____ your vision, then act in _____ on your beliefs, according to your personal philosophy. (*page 38*)

FOR FURTHER STUDY:

You confess what you believe: *"A good man out of the good treasure of his heart bringeth forth that which is good; and an evil man out of the evil treasures of his heart bringeth forth that which is evil: for out of the abundance of the heart his mouth speaketh"* (Luke 6:45).

The common bond of friends is their trust: *"A friend loveth at all times"* (Proverbs 17:17); *"Faithful re the wounds of a friend"* (Proverbs 27:6); *"Ointment and perfume rejoice the heart: so does the sweetness of a man's friend by hearty counsel"* (Proverbs 27:9).

Associations with people who will not grow can frustrate and discourage growth in your life (see Psalm 1:1–3; Romans 12:3-6): *"Be ye not unequally yoked together with unbelievers: for what fellowship hath righteousness with unrighteousness? And what communion hath light with darkness?"* (2 Corinthians 6:14); *"To them that have obtained like precious faith with us through the righteousness of God and our Saviour Jesus Christ"* (2 Peter 1:1).

N. Check True or False for the following sentences: *(pages 38–39)*

Good is the friend of best. ____True ____False

Dreams without goals go nowhere. ____True ____False

Water always seeks its own level. ____True ____False

Knowing you can do better means you've not done your best. ____True ____False

To have more, don't settle for less. ____True ____False

Every good thing in life begins with you. ____True ____False

1. You can be one of the world's thousands of _____ or one of its few
_____. *(page 38)*

2. When you live by someone's failed philosophy, you _____ his
_____. *(page 39)*

FOR FURTHER STUDY

Take responsibility to cultivate and invest your God-given talents (see Matthew 25:14–30): *"Do not neglect the gift which is in you"*
(1 Timothy 4:14 AMPC); *"Fan into flame the gift of God.... Guard the good deposit that was entrusted to you"* (2 Timothy 1:6, 14 NIV).
Determine to follow after success and godliness (see Deuteronomy 8:18; Joshua 1:7–8): *"But as for me and my house, we will serve the LORD"*
(Joshua 24:15; see also Psalm 119:46); *"The good influence of godly citizens causes a city to prosper"* (Proverbs 11:11 TLB).
A blessed man: *"His delight is in the law of the LORD; and in his law doth he meditate day and night. And he shall be like a tree planted by the
rivers of water, that bringeth forth his fruit in his season; his leaf also shall not wither; and whatsoever he doeth shall prosper"* (Psalm 1:2–3).
Refuse to accept other's failed philosophies: *"Blessed is the man that walketh not in the counsel of the ungodly, nor standeth in the way of sinners,
nor sitteth in the seat of the scornful"* (Psalm 1:1); *"Beware lest any man spoil you through philosophy and vain deceit, after the tradition of men,
after the rudiments of the world, and not after Christ"* (Colossians 2:8).

PRACTICAL:

1. "Without a vision for the future, the only vision we have is our past. That's all we can see." (*page 29*)

If this describes you, what steps should you take to improve your life?

_____

_____

_____

2. Since "no man is an island," explain the lie that says, "What a person does in private is his own business." (*pages 37*)

_____

_____

_____

REPEAT THIS PRAYER OUT LOUD:

Father, I want to dream big enough to have hope, a sense of destiny and purpose. With Your help, I will write my dreams, confess them and commit to them. I pray my perceptions align with truth so that I can be free. I know that my faith will attract the positive and that I must choose best, not settle for good. Help me make my personal philosophy pleasing to You. In Jesus's name. Amen.

PRINCIPLES I WANT TO MEMORIZE:

SELF-TEST—LESSON 2

1. A person without a vision is a person without a future. A person without a future will always return to his past.

    _____ True   _____ False

2. Knowing you can do better means you've not done your best.

    _____ True   _____ False

3. What you think in your heart determines what you _____. *(circle one)*

    have for lunch   do on vacation   become

4. Images in our minds drive us toward our _____.

5. Name four things faith attracts:

    the _____, _____, _____, and _____

6. Private philosophy determines public performance.

    _____ True   _____ False

7. Faith is _____ in _____.

8. The most powerful thing you can do in life is_____. *(circle one)*

    own a business   create an image   run for office   win the lottery

9. Good is the _____ of best.

LESSON 3
SEEK TRUE WEALTH

LESSON 3
SEEK TRUE WEALTH

A. Wealth and riches are not _____. *(page 41)*

1. Wealth will get you _____, but riches will never make you

_____. *(page 41)*

2. True wealth comes from your _____. *(page 41)*

3. Succeeding in business will always leave you fulfilled. *(page 41)*

_____ True   _____ False

4. List four things that will help give you the power to get wealth: *(page 41)*

_____   _____

_____   _____

5. Wealth is realized only when coupled with a degree of _____,

_____, _____, and _____ health. *(page 41)*

6. Business success always requires more staff, equipment, time, hard work and office space. *(pages 41–42)*

_____ True   _____ False

FOR FURTHER STUDY

God will provide for you: *"But thou shalt remember the Lord thy God: for it is he that giveth thee power to get wealth"* (Deuteronomy 8:18); *"But my God shall supply all your need according to his riches in glory by Christ Jesus"* (Philippians 4:19; see also Luke 11:9-10).
Measure success by good character, not money: *"For the Lord seeth not as man seeth; for man looketh on the outward appearance, but the Lord looketh on the heart"* (1 Samuel 16:7); *"A good name is rather to be chosen than great riches, and loving favour rather than silver and gold"* (Proverbs 22:1); *"Take heed, and beware of covetousness: for a man's life consisteth not in the abundance of things which he possesseth. …God said unto him, Thou fool…whose shall those things be"* (Luke 12:15, 20); *"Because thou sayest, I am rich, and increased with goods, and have need of nothing; and knowest not that thou art wretched, and miserable, and poor, and blind, and naked"* (Revelation 3:17).
The issue isn't being rich or poor but being obedient: *"How hard is it for them that trust in riches to enter into the kingdom of God!"* (Mark 10:24).

B. Producing riches by doing what you hate is a form of: *(circle one)* *(page 42–43)*

being humble   persevering   cheating yourself

1. Money cannot compensate for the lack of _____ _____.
(page 43)

2. You are not like anyone else on earth, and you are not supposed to be. *(page 43)*

_____True _____False

3. You can follow the principles and the pattern, but you must: *(page 43)*

accentuate your own _____

excel in your own _____

revel in what you _____ _____

celebrate your _____

4. Gifts and talents are never _____—only _____. *(page 44)*

5. Your greatest fulfillment will be found in the place where you: *(circle one)* *(page 44)*

utilize your gifts and talents   get married   earn a six-figure income

C. Most people are more aware of what they do _____ than what they do
_____. *(page 44)*

FOR FURTHER STUDY

Let God put creative ideas in your mind and godly desires in your heart and fulfill His will by enabling you to realize those dreams (see Psalm 37:4): *"For I know the thoughts and plans that I have for you, says the Lord, thoughts and plans for welfare and peace and not for evil, to give you hope in your final outcome"* (Jeremiah 29:11 AMPC).
God is the source of all: *"For from him and through him and to him are all things"* (Romans 11:36 NIV); *"And God is able to make all grace abound toward you; that ye, always having all sufficiency in all things, may abound in every good work"* (2 Corinthians 9:8); *"Every good gift and every perfect gift is from above, and cometh down from the Father of lights"* (James 1:17).
Use riches wisely: *"If riches increase, set not your heart upon them"* (Psalm 62:10); *"But godliness with contentment is great gain. …For the love of money is the root of all evil: which while some coveted after…. Be not highminded, nor trust in uncertain riches, but in the living God, who giveth us richly all things to enjoy"* (1 Timothy 6:6, 10, 17); *"I have learned, in whatsoever state I am, therewith to be content"* (Philippians 4:11; see also Jude 11).

---

1. Weaknesses need not have power over strengths. *(page 44)*

_____ True   _____ False

2. Strengths are always tainted by weaknesses. *(page 44)*

_____ True   _____ False

3. Spending all your time on your weaknesses guarantees you will become: *(circle one)* *(page 44)*

successful   a dull boy   average   stronger

4. Clues to finding your strengths: *(circle all that apply)* *(page 44–45)*

what someone will pay you a lot of money to do

what you want to do during recreation and relaxation

what stirs your creative juices

what your spouse wants you to do

what fills your waking thoughts

D.   All of life depends on _____. *(page 45)*

1. Why should you "find someone with strengths in the areas of your weaknesses"? *(pages 45)*

_____

_____

FOR FURTHER STUDY

Concentrate on your strengths, not your weaknesses: "*God has given each of us the ability to do certain things well*" (Romans 12:6 TLB).
To become a champion, you must see yourself as a champion: "*I can do all things through Christ which strengtheneth me*" (Philippians 4:13).
When a man honors God, he strengthens his character, increases the stature of his manhood, and finds favor with God and man: "*The righteous also shall hold on his way, and he that hath clean hands shall be stronger and stronger*" (Job 17:9; see also Psalm 84:5, 7; 89:17; Proverbs 4:18); "*Increased in wisdom and stature, and in favour with God and man*" (Luke 2:52; see also verse 40).
Friendship is normal to life: "*Two are better than one.... For if they fall, the one will lift up his fellow: but woe to him that is alone when he falleth; for he hath not another to help him up*" (Ecclesiastes 4:9–10); "*A friend loveth at all times*" (Proverbs 17:17); "*A man that hath friends must show himself friendly*" (Proverbs 18:24); "*Faithful are the wounds of a friend.... Iron sharpeneth iron; so a man sharpeneth the countenance of his friend*" (Proverbs 27:6, 17).

2. List five primary factors in achieving success: *(page 47)*

C_____ _____

I_____—not just education but _____ _____

I_____

E_____

A positive _____

E.   These three things sabotage success: *(page 47)*

Lust of the _____

Lust of the _____

Pride of _____

1. True humility is simply the willingness to remain _____. *(page 47)*

2. "There is no limit to the _____ a _____ can do if he doesn't care who gets the _____." *(page 47)*

3. Overcoming _____ opens the door for you to start over on the next level. *(circle one) (page 49)*

defeat   poverty   pride   fear   power

FOR FURTHER STUDY

Great by wealth of virtue: *"The good influence of godly citizens causes a city to prosper, but the moral decay of the wicked drives it downhill"* (Proverbs 11:11 TLB); *"He that trusteth in his riches shall fall: but the righteous shall flourish as a branch"* (Proverbs 11:28); *"Righteousness exalteth a nation"* (Proverbs 14:34); *"Take heed, and beware of covetousness: for a man's life consisteth not in the abundance of the things which he possesseth"* (Luke 12:15).

Covetous vs. Generous: *"It is possible to give away and become richer! It is also possible to hold on too tightly and lose everything. Yes, the liberal man shall be rich! By watering others, he waters himself"* (Proverbs 11:24-25 TLB; see also Proverbs 28:27).

Love is a characteristic of God's kingdom (see John 3:16): *"Herein is love, not that we loved God, but that he loved us, and sent his Son to be the propitiation for our sins"* (1 John 4:9–10).

Lust is a characteristic of Satan's kingdom: *"Ye are of your father the devil, and the lusts of your father ye will do"* (John 8:44; see also Proverbs 27:20; 1 John 2:16).

Pride: *"Pride goeth before destruction, and an haughty spirit before a fall"* (Proverbs 16:18).

F. Write the correct letter in the blank that completes the sentence. *(page 49)*

____ Lust is just perverted   a. law

____ The emotional opposite of love is   b. lust

____ The legal opposite of love is   c. love

____ The moral opposite of love is   d. hate

1. Love is the desire to benefit _____ at the expense of _____, because love desires to _____. *(page 49)*

2. Lust is the desire to benefit _____ even at the expense of _____, because lust desires to _____. *(page 49)*

3. Lust always pertains to a sexual dynamic between men and women. *(page 49)*

____ True   ____ False

4. _____ is easily satisfied. _____ has no limits and can find no ends. *(page 50)*

5. _____ determines civilization. *(circle one) (page 51)*

   Fashion   Money   Culture   Education   Government

6. Give three examples of how employees lust their jobs: *(page 51)*

_____

_____

_____

FOR FURTHER STUDY

Commanded to love: *"Jesus said unto him…. Thou shalt love thy neighbour as thyself"* (Matthew 22:37, 39); *"The goal of this command is love, which comes from a pure heart and a good conscience and a sincere faith"* (1 Timothy 1:5 NIV); *"Love worketh no ill to his neighbour: therefore love is the fulfilling of the law"* (Romans 13:10); *"Let every one of us please his neighbour for his good to edification"* (Romans 15:2).

Money can bring temptation, worry (see Proverbs 15:27; 18:11; Isaiah 1:23): *"The cares of this world, and the deceitfulness of riches"* (Mark 4:19); *"They that will be rich fall into temptation and a snare, and into many foolish and hurtful lusts, which drown men in destruction and perdition"* (1 Timothy 6:9; see also 2 Peter 2:15).

Talkers vs. Producers (see Proverbs 12:11; 13:4, 11): *"Work brings profit; talk brings poverty!"* (Proverbs 14:23 TLB); *"He also that is slothful in his work is brother to him that is a great waster"* (Proverbs 18:9); *"By much slothfulness the building decayeth; and through idleness of the hands the house droppeth through"* (Ecclesiastes 10:18; see also Luke 19:20–22).

7. List three ways to operate in love for your body: (*page 52*)

Take care of your _____

Eat _____

Maintain an _____ _____

G. On the pathway to prosperity: (*page 53*)

guard _____, avoid the three basic _____, and control your

_____.

H. "Master your _____ or your _____ will master you." (*page 53*)

I. Write the correct letter in the blank that completes the sentence. (*pages 53–54*)

_____Focus on your strengths so your weaknesses become   a. blessing.

_____Humility precedes   b. equally.

_____When you find your strengths, you find your path to total life   c. irrelevant.

_____Love is easily satisfied. Lust is   d. insatiable.

_____God created each of us uniquely but not   e. prosperity.

FOR FURTHER STUDY

How to live: "*A sound heart is the life of the flesh: but envy the rottenness of the bones*" (Proverbs 14:30; see also Isaiah 43:2); "*Do not be anxious about anything*" Philippians 4:6 NIV); "*So whoever cleanses himself [from what is ignoble and unclean, who separates himself from contact with contaminating and corrupting influences] will [then himself] be a vessel set apart and useful for honorable and noble purposes, consecrated and profitable to the Master, fit and ready for any good work*" (2 Timothy 2:21 AMPC); "*A person who is pure of heart sees goodness and purity in everything; but a person whose own heart is evil and untrusting finds evil in everything, for his dirty mind and rebellious heart color all he sees and hears. Such persons claim they know God, but from seeing the way they act, one knows they don't. They are rotten and disobedient, worthless so far as doing anything good is concerned*" (Titus 1:15, 16 TLB).
Imitate Christ's humility. (See Philippians 2:1–11.)

J. It takes humility to: *(page 48)*

admit what you don't _____

admit _____

_____ again.

_____

K. Love is the nature of _____. Lust is the nature of _____. *(page 50)*

L. _____ is the folly of youth.

_____ is the folly of old age.

_____ is the folly of middle age. *(page 48)*

M. Love is exhibited by working for someone's highest good. *(page 51)*

_____ True _____ False

FOR FURTHER STUDY

A good, wise man (see Joshua 22:5): *"A good man out of the good treasure of his heart bringeth forth that which is good"* (Luke 6:45); *"Study to show thyself approved unto God, a workman that needeth not to be ashamed, rightly dividing the word of truth"* (2 Timothy 2:15); *"Who is a wise man and endued with knowledge among you? let him show out of a good conversation his works with meekness of wisdom"* (James 3:13).
Humility (see Deuteronomy 8:2–3, 16; 2 Kings 5; 2 Chronicles 7:14; Proverbs 15:33; 18:12): *"Humble yourselves in the sight of the Lord, and he shall lift you up"* (James 4:10; see also 1 Peter 5:5–6).
Exhibit love: *"Love endures long and is patient and kind; love never is envious nor boils over with jealousy, is not boastful or vainglorious, does not display itself haughtily. It is not conceited (arrogant and inflated with pride); it is not rude (unmannerly) and does not act unbecomingly. Love (God's love in us) does not insist on its own rights or its own way, for it is not self-seeking; it is not touchy or fretful or resentful; it takes no account of the evil done to it [it pays no attention to a suffered wrong]"* (1 Corinthians 13:4, 5 AMPC).

PRACTICAL:

1. What is "hardening of the attitudes"? What "cures" this "illness"? *(page 48)*

_____

_____

_____

_____

2. How can temptation sabotage you and end your quest for prosperity? *(page 52)*

_____

_____

_____

_____

REPEAT THIS PRAYER OUT LOUD:

Father, in Jesus's name, help me discover and exercise my God-given gifts and talents to achieve the goals you have for me. Help me avoid the pitfalls that threaten to sabotage my success. With Your grace, I commit to be humble, to exhibit love, to build relationships with people who bring balance to my life, to master my passions. Amen.

_____

PRINCIPLES I WANT TO MEMORIZE:

SELF-TEST—LESSON 3

1. Love always desires to benefit _____ at the expense of _____.

   Lust desires to benefit _____ at the expense of _____.

2. Gifts and talents are never earned, only discovered.

   _____True _____False

3. True wealth comes from your _____.

4. Name five primary factors in achieving success:

   _____

   _____

   _____

   _____

   _____

5. Wealth will get you _____, but riches will never make you _____.

6. Spending all your time on your weaknesses guarantees you will become: *(circle one)*

   successful   a dull boy   average   stronger

7. Money cannot compensate for the lack of _____ _____.

8. All of life depends on relationships.

   _____True _____False

9. Humility precedes _____.

10. True humility is simply the willingness to remain _____.

LESSON 4
CHARACTER COUNTS

LESSON 4
CHARACTER COUNTS

A.   It is always easier to _____ than to _____. *(page 55)*

    1. It is possible for your talent to take you to a place where your _____ cannot _____ you. *(page 55)*

    2. Character is always more important than talent. *(page 56)*

        ____ True   ____ False

    3. People can commit to _____. They cannot commit to _____. *(page 56)*

B.   Write the correct letter in the blank that completes the sentence. *(page 56)*

____Character is an internal quality	a. checks and balances from without.
____Character has no self-creative powers	b. it is fed from external sources.
____The best character is in constant need of	c. nor any self-corrective power.
____Character deteriorates over time unless	d. that is fed by external sources.

    1. The _____ of the external sources that character feeds on determines its _____. *(page 56)*

    2. List two externals that help build or destroy character: *(page 57)*

_____   _____

FOR FURTHER STUDY

Maintain: "*It is required in stewards, that a man be found faithful*" (1 Corinthians 4:2).

When a man honors God, his character increases: "*The righteous shall move onward and forward; those with pure hearts shall become stronger and stronger*" (Job 17:9 TLB; see also Psalm 84:5, 7; 89:17; Proverbs 4:18); "*I have refrained my feet from every evil way.... I have not departed from thy judgments: for thou hast taught me. ...Through thy precepts I get understanding: therefore I hate every false way*" Psalm 119:101–102, 104; see also Luke 2:40, 52.)

God commits to character, not talent: "*Well done, thou good and faithful servant: thou hast been faithful over a few things, I will make thee ruler over many things: enter thou into the joy of thy lord*" (Matthew 25:21); "*Faithful in that which is least is faithful also in much*" (Luke 16:10); "*Things you have heard me say...entrust to reliable men who will also be qualified to teach others*" (2 Timothy 2:2 NIV).

Our choices are shown by the company we keep: "*A mirror reflects a man's face, but what he is really like is shown by the kind of friends he chooses*" (Proverbs 27:19 TLB).

3. Evil companionships corrupt good character. *(page 57)*

_____ True   _____ False

4. Write the correct letter in the blank that completes the sentence. *(page 57)*

_____Quality is always determined internally   a. the higher the gloss.

_____Real quality in material or character   b. never externally.

_____The cheaper the merchandise   c. the internal shines through.

_____Externals reveal what is internal, and   d. needs nothing to cover it up.

5. Good character requires: *(page 57)*

no _____, no _____

no _____, no _____

C. _____is king in character, the only moral, _____and
_____foundation for good character. *(page 57)*

1. The way to build good character is to base it upon your beliefs about _____,
_____, _____, and _____. *(page 57–58)*

2. To develop good character, truth must be: *(page 58)*

_____   _____

_____   _____

FOR FURTHER STUDY

Invest in character: *"A good name is rather to be chosen than great riches"* (Proverbs 22:1); *"You are not to keep company with anyone who claims to be a brother Christian but indulges in sexual sins, or is greedy, or is a swindler…. Don't even eat lunch with such a person"* (1 Corinthians 5:11 TLB); *"Do not be yoked together with unbelievers. For what do righteousness and wickedness have in common? Or what fellowship can light have with darkness?...let us purify ourselves from everything that contaminates body and spirit, perfecting holiness out of reverence for God"* (2 Corinthians 6:14; 7:1; 2 Peter 1:5–7).

Integrity: Firm adherence to a code of especially moral values; incorruptibility.

Be a man of integrity: *"I beg you…to live and act in a way worthy of those who have been chosen for such wonderful blessings as these"* (Ephesians 4:1 TLB).

Don't submit your personal character to that of your peer group (see Exodus 23:2–3; Psalm 16:3 TLB): *"Do not be misled: 'Bad company corrupts good character'"* (1 Corinthians 15:33 NIV).

3. Check True or False for the following sentences: *(pages 58)*

Strongly-held opinions will hold up to truth.	____ True	____ False
Truth is the rock upon which we build good character.	____ True	____ False
Without good character, all accomplishments are short-lived.	____ True	____ False
Trust is extended to the limit of truth and no more.	____ True	____ False
A partner who is rarely dishonest can sometimes be trusted.	____ True	____ False
Trusting in a half truth is trusting in a whole lie.	____ True	____ False

4. We must learn _____, _____ on it and hold it as a valued and cherished _____ in order to _____ and _____ strong character that translates into _____ order and peaceful _____ living. *(use words from the following list) (page 58)*

corporate   treasure   develop   trust   meditate   truth   societal   maintain

D.   Political elections and beleaguered corporations use "_____" to tell their version of "_____," which is overall a euphemism for "_____." *(page 59)*

1. Honesty is an issue, because when truth collapses, morality has nothing on which to stand. *(page 59)*

____ True   ____ False

FOR FURTHER STUDY

Character is built in private, developed out of a lifetime of individual decisions which either enhance or diminish it: *"I have chosen the way of truth: thy judgments have I laid before me"* (Psalm 119:30); *"If a man therefore purge himself from these, he shall be a vessel unto honour, sanctified, and meet for the master's use, and prepared unto every good work"* (2 Timothy 2:21).

Have character, be faithful: *"Well done, thou good and faithful servant: thou hast been faithful over a few things, I will make thee ruler over many things: enter thou into the joy of thy Lord"* (Matthew 25:21); *"He that is faithful in that which is least is faithful also in much"* (Luke 16:10; see also 2 Timothy 2:2).

Moral courage enables a person to encounter hatred, disapproval and contempt without departing from what is right: *"Many are my persecutors and my adversaries, yet I do not swerve from Your testimonies"* (Psalm 119:157 AMPC).

Examples of moral courage: Gideon (see Judges 6–7); David (see 1 Samuel 17); Daniel (see Daniel 6); John the Baptist (see Matthew 14:3–10); Stephen (see Acts 7); Paul (see Acts 27; 28:1–6).

2. The collapse of truth brings disaster: *(page 59)*

_____ and economically, both individually and _____ .

3. Individual and national character is founded upon truth. *(page 59)*

_____ True   _____ False

4. People and nations are not great by _____ of their _____ but by the _____ of their _____ . *(page 59)*

5. Truth stands the test of time. *(page 61)*

_____ True   _____ False

6. If you've made a mistake, _____ _____ _____ _____ right away. Never try to lie your way out of anything. *(page 61)*

7. In general, commerce, industry and business are accomplished by _____ . *(page 63)*

8. What is the reward of the trustworthy? *(page 63)*

_____

9. List three rewards of telling the truth: *(page 63)*

_____ of _____ , _____ from _____ , and _____ of _____ .

FOR FURTHER STUDY

Truth is the bedrock of integrity which is the cornerstone of individual and national character: *"I want the company of the godly men and women in the land; they are the true nobility"* (Psalm 16:3 TLB; see also Psalm 24:4–5; Zechariah 8:16); *"The good influence of godly citizens causes a city to prosper, but the moral decay of the wicked drives it downhill. …Without wise leadership, a nation is in trouble"* (Proverbs 11:11, 14 TLB); *"When there is moral rot within a nation, its government topples easily; but with honest, sensible leaders there is stability"* (Proverbs 28:2 TLB); *"With good men in authority, the people rejoice…with the wicked in power, they groan"* (Proverbs 29:2 TLB; see also Matthew 7:15–16). Admit mistakes: *"A man who refuses to admit his mistakes can never be successful. But if he confesses and forsakes them, he gets another chance"* (Proverbs 28:13 TLB).

The characteristics of the kingdom emanate from the character of the king: *"'Like priests, like people'—because the priests are wicked, the people are too"* (Hosea 4:9 TLB).

E. The truth is always _____, and a lie is always _____.
_____ must _____ our heart of _____. Any untruth is _____ on _____ grounds and _____ for _____ reasons. *(use words from the following list) (page 63–65)*

occupy   personal   wrong   social   hearts   immoral   right   truth   illegitimate

1. There is nothing _____, _____, or good in a person who lies. *(page 65)*

2. A person who chooses to believes lies, when he knows the truth in his heart, is _____. *(page 65)*

F. Write the correct letter in the blank that completes the sentence. *(pages 65-66)*

_____When it comes to winning at life, the heart comes   a. vital.

_____Our creed is   b. absolute.

_____The acid test of character is in your   c. matter.

_____Our beliefs are   d. basic.

_____Truth is the only   e. first.

_____Our thoughts   f. heart.

FOR FURTHER STUDY

A man's word and character (see Proverbs 21:8; 24:3–4): *"A good man out of the good treasure of his heart bringeth forth that which is good…for out of the abundance of the heart his mouth speaketh"* (Luke 6:45).

A man's name is only as good as his word: *"In many ways we offend all. If any man offend not in word, the same is a perfect man, and able also to bridle the whole body"* (James 3:2).

Prepare your name to have a good character: *"A truthful witness gives honest testimony, but a false witness tells lies"* (Proverbs 12:17 NIV).

Choose a good name: *"A good name is rather to be chosen than great riches, and loving favour rather than silver and gold"* (Proverbs 22:1); *"A good name is better than fine perfume"* (Ecclesiastes 7:1 NIV).

Choose character: *"Her husband is respected at the city gate…. A woman who fears the LORD is to be praised. …Let her works bring her praise at the city gate"* (Proverbs 31:23, 30– 31 NIV).

G. Whatever you _____, _____, and concentrate on will eventually drop from your _____ to your _____. *(page 65)*

1. The issues of life spring from your heart. *(page 65)*

    _____ True   _____ False

2. What is in your heart will bring you _____ or _____, _____ or _____. *(page 65)*

3. In the womb, our _____ are created first, then our _____. *(page 65)*

4. If our minds are the _____ _____, our hearts are the _____ _____. *(page 65)*

5. _____, creeds, and _____ feed our heart and program it to propel us toward _____ and to believe what our _____ may not be able to conceive. *(page 66)*

6. You can pitch your _____, but you _____ your _____. *(page 66)*

FOR FURTHER STUDY

Personality is not the same as character: *"Pretty words may hide a wicked heart, just as a pretty glaze covers a common clay pot"* (Proverbs 26:23 TLB).

Personality is after the outward man and is temporal: *"For the LORD seeth not as man seeth; for man looketh on the outward appearance, but the LORD looketh on the heart"* (1 Samuel 16:7).

Your heart: *"Keep thy heart with all diligence…out of it are the issues of life"* (Proverbs 4:23); *"A good man out of the good treasure of his heart bringeth forth that which is good; and an evil man out of the evil treasure of his heart bringeth forth that which is evil: for of the abundance of the heart his mouth speaketh"* (Luke 6:45).

Lay a right foundation for your character: *"Since we have these promises…let us purify ourselves from everything that contaminates body and spirit, perfecting holiness out of reverence for God"* (2 Corinthians 7:1 NIV; Proverbs 21:8; 24:3–4; 31:23, 30–31 AMPC).

H. Check True or False for the following sentences: *(pages 66–67)*

Your talent can take you where your character can't sustain you. _____ True _____ False

You can tell a person's character by the company he keeps. _____ True _____ False

Good character overrides evil companionships. _____ True _____ False

Quality is always determined internally, never externally. _____ True _____ False

Trusting in a half truth is trusting in a whole lie. _____ True _____ False

People and nations are great by the virtue of their wealth. _____ True _____ False

The truth is always right, and a lie is always wrong. _____ True _____ False

You can pitch your personality, but you build your character. _____ True _____ False

I. Using the following words, complete these sentences. *(pages 66–67)*

mind   truth   become   character   obtain   trustworthy   heart   trust   maintain

It is always easier to _____ than to _____.

_____ is extended to the limit of truth and no more.

When _____ collapses, morality has nothing on which to stand.

The reward of the _____ is more trust.

Your _____ can believe what your _____ cannot conceive.

What you think in your heart determines what you _____.

When the charm wears off, you have nothing but _____ left.

FOR FURTHER STUDY:

Maturation is a lifelong process: *"You, therefore, must be perfect [growing into complete maturity of godliness in mind and character, having reached the proper height of virtue and integrity], as your heavenly Father is perfect"* (Matthew 10:48 AMPC); *"We also rejoice in our sufferings, because we know that suffering produces perseverance; perseverance, character; and character, hope"* (Romans 5:3–5 NIV); *"We are more than conquerors through him that loved us"* (Romans 8:37); *"Let us not be weary in well doing: for in due season we shall reap, if we faint not"* (Galatians 6:9).
Renew your mind: *"Lie not…seeing that ye have put off the old man…and have put on the new man"* (Colossians 3:9–10); *"And be not conformed to this world: but be ye transformed by the renewing of your mind, that ye may prove what is that good, and acceptable, and perfect, will of God"* (Romans 12:2); *"Be renewed in the spirit of your mind"* (Ephesians 4:23); *"Let this mind be in you, which was also in Christ Jesus"* (Philippians 2:5).

PRACTICAL:

1. "We each have the option of adapting to the culture around us—which values the license to lie above the liberty to walk in truth." *(page 63)*

   Explain the effects such a decision has on society and you personally.

   Society: _____

   _____

   Me: _____

   _____

2. Headlines routinely cite examples of people who pitched their personalities but failed to build their character. In what ways might you be "pitching" rather than "building"? What action will you take to remedy this?

   _____

   _____

   _____

REPEAT THIS PRAYER OUT LOUD:

Father, thank You for the gifts and talents You've given me. I ask for wisdom and discipline so my character can maintain them. I commit to spend time with good reading material and godly people, to seek after, study out, learn and rehearse truth—to build my character, in Jesus's name. Amen.

FOR FURTHER STUDY

Choices determine conduct, character and destiny: "*My son, if sinners entice you, do not give in to them. If they say, 'Come along with us…cast lots with us'…do not go along with them, do not set foot on their paths; for their feet rush into evil, they are swift to shed blood*" (Proverbs 1:10–16 NIV); "*A good man is known by his truthfulness; a false man by deceit and lies…No real harm befalls the good, but there is constant trouble for the wicked*" (Proverbs 12:17, 21 TLB); "*Be with wise men and become wise. Be with evil men and become evil*" (Proverbs 13:20 TLB); "*Walk with the wise and become wise, for a companion of fools suffers harm*" (Proverbs 13:20 NIV); "*Run from anything that gives you the evil thoughts that young men often have, but stay close to anything that makes you want to do right*" (2 Timothy 2:22 TLB).

SELF-TEST—LESSON 4

1. Build good character by basing it upon your beliefs about:

    _____   _____

    _____   _____

2. It is possible for your talent to take you to a place where your _____ _____ _____ _____.

3. Complete the following statements:

    a. To trust in a half truth is to trust in a _____ _____.

    b. It is always easier to _____ than to _____.

    c. Evil companionships _____ good character.

    d. Your _____ can believe what your _____ cannot conceive.

4. Strongly-held opinions will hold up to truth.   ____ True   ____ False

5. The issues of life spring from your heart.   ____ True   ____ False

6. List three rewards of telling the truth:

    _____

    _____

    _____

7. Trust is extended to the limit of truth and no more.   ____ True   ____ False

8. You can pitch your _____, but you _____ your _____.

9. People and nations are not great by _____ of their _____ but by the _____ of their _____.

LESSON 5
THE NATURE OF MONEY

LESSON 5
THE NATURE OF MONEY

A. The use of your money reveals your _____ that come from your
_____. *(page 69)*

1. To see where your heart is, open your _____. *(page 69)*

2. *In your own words*, describe how money represents your life: *(page 69)*

_____

_____

3. How you spend your money shows what you do with your life. *(page 69)*

____True   ____False

4. If you want your life to count, make your _____ count. Master the
_____ that master money. *(page 69)*

B. Sum up the traditional American work ethic in one phrase: *(page 69)*

_____

1. Explain how that work ethic is being threatened today: *(pages 69–70)*

_____

_____

FOR FURTHER STUDY

Work!: *"The wages of the righteous is life, but the earnings of the wicked are sin and punishment"* (Proverbs 10:16 NIV); *"Lazy people want much but get little, while the diligent are prospering"* (Proverbs 13:4 TLB); *"Work brings profit; talk brings poverty!"* (Proverbs 14:23 TLB); *"Dishonest gain will never last, so why take the risk?"* (Proverbs 21:6 TLB); *"If any would not work, neither should he eat"* (2 Thessalonians 3:10). Gambling: *"Ill-gotten gain brings no lasting happiness; right living does"* (Proverbs 10:2 TLB); *"Wealth from gambling quickly disappears; wealth from hard work grows"* (Proverbs 13:11 TLB); *"Wealth gotten by vanity shall be diminished: but he that gathereth by labour shall increase"* (Proverbs 13:11); *"Steady plodding brings prosperity; hasty speculation brings poverty"* (Proverbs 21:5 TLB); *"The man who wants to do right will get a rich reward. But the man who wants to get rich quick will quickly fail"* (Proverbs 28:20 TLB); *"Trying to get rich quick is evil and leads to poverty"* (Proverbs 28:22 TLB).

2. Winning the lottery insures lifetime financial security. (*page 70*)

_____ True   _____ False

Why?

_____

3. _____ is the priority in business. (*page 70*)

4. The number one way to making a profit is: (*circle one*) (*page 70*)

   always using a locally-owned bank.

   serving the customer properly.

   cutting costs with lower quality and higher prices.

5. Learn to meet a need, and money will follow. (*page 70*)

_____ True   _____ False

6. In sales, you're never selling a product but an _____ to a _____.
(*page 70*)

C. Complete this sentence using the following words: (pages 71)

   financial   truth   characters   prosper   words   encouraging   prosperity

   "If we feed our minds and hearts and program our _____ with

   _____ and _____ _____, our hearts and minds

   will start to _____ and external _____ _____

   will come."

FOR FURTHER STUDY

Get rich quick schemes: *"Wealth [not earned but] won in haste or unjustly or from the production of things for vain or detrimental use [such riches] will dwindle away, but he who gathers little by little will increase [his riches]"* (Proverbs 13:11 AMPC).

Be a servant/meet a need: *"For they gave me respite from labor and rested me and refreshed my spirit as well as yours. Deeply appreciate and thoroughly know and fully recognize such men"* (1 Corinthians 16:18 AMPC); *"Your love has given me great joy and encouragement, because you… have refreshed the hearts of the Lord's people"* (Philemon 7 NIV).

Right living results in prosperity: *"This should be your ambition: to live a quiet life, minding your own business and doing your own work…. As a result, people who are not Christians will trust and respect you, and you will not need to depend on others for enough money to pay your bills"* (1 Thessalonians 4:11–12 TLB).

---

1. Name the "three critical Es": *(page 71)*

_____, _____ , and _____

2. Before you ever become a success in business, you must become a success in your own heart. *(page 71)*

_____ True _____ False

3. No amount of money can overcome a poverty spirit produced by what two things? *(page 71)*

Fearing the _____

Thinking only of _____

4. Loving money ensures: *(circle one) (page 71)*

you'll have enough for retirement.

you'll be motivated to keep producing.

you'll never have enough money.

5. Lasting prosperity is first in _____ , then in _____. *(page 72)*

D. How is poverty being propelled and propagated in American society? *(page 72)*

_____

1. Co-signing makes us servants to another person's debt. *(page 72)*

_____ True _____ False

FOR FURTHER STUDY

Money and business (see Luke 12:16–20): *"A greedy person is really an idol worshiper—he loves and worships the good things of this life more than God"* (Ephesians 5:5 TLB).

Man gives money value: *"For the love of money is the root of all evil: which while some coveted after, they have erred from the faith, and pierced themselves through with many sorrows. …Charge them that are rich in this world, that they be not highminded, nor trust in uncertain riches, but in the living God, who giveth us richly all things to enjoy"* (1 Timothy 6:10, 17; see also Hebrews 12:16; 1 Peter 2:15; Jude 11).

Money can bring temptation and worry: *"If you endorse a note for someone you hardly know, guaranteeing his debt, you are in serious trouble. …Quick! Get out of it if you possibly can! …If you can get out of this trap you have saved yourself"* (Proverbs 6:1, 3, 5 TLB); *"Whoever puts up security for a stranger will surely suffer, but whoever refuses to shake hands in pledge is safe"* (Proverbs 11:15 NIV); *"But they that will be rich fall into temptation and a snare, and into many foolish and hurtful lusts"* (Proverbs 15:27; see also Isaiah 1:23; 1 Timothy 6:9; 2 Peter 2:15).

2. Good debt management stems from: *(circle one)* *(page 72)*

mastering the checkbook   MasterCard   mastering our passions

3. In your own words, how has debt become a modern form of slavery? *(page 72)*

_____

_____

4. "_____ _____" are created when an entire group buys into a particular temptation. *(page 72)*

5. Temptations to do wrong always promise on the surface to _____ and _____ but only desire to _____ and _____. When the pleasure is gone, the _____ can last for a _____ or an _____. *(page 72)*

6. People are negative by nature and have to be converted to the positive. *(page 73)*

_____ True   _____ False

7. Winning the debt battle requires what two things? *(page 74)*

_____   _____

8. Every level of life is achieved _____. *(page 75)*

FOR FURTHER STUDY

Be clear with debtors: *"Don't withhold repayment of your debts. Don't say 'some other time,' if you can pay now"* (Proverbs 3:27–28 TLB); *"Do things in such a way that everyone can see you are honest clear through"* (Romans 12:17 TLB).

Debt enslaves: *"Just as the rich rule the poor, so the borrower is servant to the lender"* (Proverbs 22:7 TLB); *"No man can serve two masters: for either he will hate the one, and love the other; or else he will hold to the one, and despise the other. Ye cannot serve God and mammon"* (Matthew 6:24); *"While they promise them liberty, they themselves are the servants of corruption: for of whom a man is overcome, of the same is he brought in bondage"* (2 Peter 2:19).

Get out of debt: *"Owe no man anything, but to love one another: for he that loveth another hath fulfilled the law"* (Romans 13:8); *"Be not entangled again with the yoke of bondage"* (Galatians 5:1).

E.   Your life can be summed up in these three words: *(page 76)*

_____, _____, _____

1. You do not own what you possess; you are only the steward of it. *(page 76)*

_____ True   _____ False

2. One of the greatest errors we make in stewardship is in our _____. The principle is "_____ _____." *(page 76)*

3. Getting out of debt before you start giving is a sound stewardship principle. *(page 76–77)*

_____ True   _____ False

4. What causes people to stumble over giving? *(page 77)*

They worry about how the _____ will be _____.

5. List two easy principles that will help you decide how to give: *(page 77)*

Give _____ __ _____ _____.

Take _____ ___ _____ _____.

6. Two things always make people happy: *(page 79)*

Receiving a _____ from _____

Giving to _____

7. _____ of _____ allows for enlarging your business. *(page 79)*

FOR FURTHER STUDY

Jesus cares how people use money: *"A certain poor widow...threw in two mites"* (Mark 12:41); *"Jesus said unto him, If thou wilt be perfect, go and sell that thou hast, and give to the poor, and thou shalt have treasure in heaven: and come and follow me"* (Matthew 19:21); *"Zacchaeus said...half of my goods I give to the poor...if I have taken...by false accusation, I restore him fourfold"* (Luke 19:8; see also Acts 5:1–2).

Covetous vs. Generous: *"It is possible to give away and become richer! It is also possible to hold on too tightly and lose everything. Yes, the liberal man shall be rich! By watering others, he waters himself"* (Proverbs 11:24–25 TLB; see also Colossians 3:5); *"He that is greedy of gain troubleth his own house"* (Proverbs 15:27; see also Proverbs 28:27).

We cannot out give God: *"Give, and it shall be given unto you; good measure, pressed down, and shaken together, and running over, shall men give into your bosom"* (Luke 6:38).

Your life is in your giving. (See Proverbs 11:24–25; Luke 21:1–5; Matthew 6:33; 10:39; 20:28.)

F.   Write the correct letter next to the word that completes the sentence. *(pages 80–83)*

_____Your care for others   a. give than to receive.

_____It is more blessed to   b. is the measure of your greatness.

_____Greatness is measured   c. buy with money.

_____You gain by giving what you cannot   d. by serving.

1. From the book, name the four things can you gain by giving. *(page 80)*

_____   _____

_____   _____

2. _____ is as important as believing. *(page 82)*

3. Answers for your needs will always come through _____. *(page 82)*

4. Success can be sabotaged by refusing _____, or being too _____ to accept their _____. *(page 82)*

G.   If you are faithful in _____, you will be faithful with _____.

You qualify for _____ by how you deal with _____.

If you are faithful in that which belongs to _____, you qualify to have that which is _____ _____. You reap what you _____. *(page 82–83)*

FOR FURTHER STUDY

Servants of money: *"No man can serve two masters: for either he will hate the one, and love the other; or else he will hold to the one, and despise the other. Ye cannot serve God and mammon"* (Matthew 6:24); *"Just as the rich rule the poor, so the borrower is servant to the lender"* (Proverbs 22:7 TLB; see also Luke 21:34).
We are only qualified to lead to the degree we are willing to serve: *"Whosoever will be great among you, let him be your minister; And whosoever will be chief among you, let him be your servant"* (Matthew 20:25–28); *"But he that is greatest among you shall be your servant"* (Matthew 23:11); *"Jesus knew their thoughts, so he stood a little child beside him and said to them, 'Anyone who takes care of a little child like this is caring for me! And whoever cares for me is caring for God who sent me. Your care for others is the measure of your greatness'"* (Luke 9:47–48 TLB); *"I am among you as he that serveth"* (Luke 22:25–27); *"Wash one another's feet. For I have given you an example"* (John 13:14–15).

---

1. The principle of investing is that by use, you _____ and _____ ;
by disuse, you _____ and _____ . *(page 83)*

2. You add by _____ , but you multiply by _____ .
_____ is simply gaining by trading. *(page 83–84)*

3. You never invest in a company, corporation or business but always in the _____
_____ _____ . *(page 84)*

4. To experience financial freedom, you must learn to live without debt. *(page 85)*

_____ True   _____ False

5. You sow to the _____ and reap from the _____ . *(page 85)*

6. Too many people buy things they _____ _____ with money
they _____ _____ to impress people they _____
_____ . *(page 85)*

7. Financial poverty springs from spiritual poverty in the heart. *(page 86)*

_____ True   _____ False

FOR FURTHER STUDY

By use you gain; by disuse you lose: *"Because thou hast been faithful in a very little, have thou authority over ten cities"* (Luke 19:17); *"Unto every one which hath shall be given...from him that hath not, even that he hath shall be taken away from him"* (Luke 19:26).

Live within your means: *"For where your treasure is, there will your heart be also"* (Matthew 6:21); *"Therefore take no thought, saying, What shall we eat? or, What shall we drink? or, Wherewithal shall we be clothed?...for your heavenly Father knoweth that ye have need of all these things"* (Matthew 6:31–32); *"Take heed, and beware of covetousness: for a man's life consisteth not in the abundance of things which he possesseth"* (Luke 12:15); *"Do not be anxious about anything"* (Philippians 4:6 NIV); *"But godliness with contentment is great gain"* (1 Timothy 6:6); *"Stay away from the love of money; be satisfied with what you have. For God has said, 'I will never, never fail you nor forsake you'"* (Hebrews 13:5 TLB).

H.   List ten investment principles: (*pages 54–85*)

1. Invest in _____.

2. Before investing, _____.

3. Risk, don't _____.

4. It must be in _____.

5. Don't _____ _____ _____.

6. Invest in _____.

7. Shadows are more _____ than _____.

8. Funds come from _____.

9. Invest your _____ for your _____ _____.

10. Don't _____.

FOR FURTHER STUDY

Put it in writing: *"In everyday life a promise made by one man to another, if it is written down and signed, cannot be changed"* (Galatians 3:15 TLB; see also Nehemiah 9:38).

Produce results or be cut off: *"Every tree that does not produce good fruit will be chopped down and thrown into the fire"* (Luke 3:7–9 TLB).

Don't avoid reality: *"He shall not be afraid of evil tidings: his heart is fixed, trusting in the Lord"* (Psalm 112:7); *"Peace I leave with you, my peace I give unto you: not as the world giveth, give I unto you. Let not your heart be troubled, neither let it be afraid"* (John 14:27); *"And the peace of God, which passeth all understanding, shall keep your hearts and minds through Christ Jesus"* (Philippians 4:7).

Friends fund: *"Never abandon a friend—either yours or your father's. Then you won't need to go to a distant relative for help in your time of need"* (Proverbs 27:10 TLB).

Don't quit: *"And let us not be weary in well doing: for in due season we shall reap, if we faint not"* (Galatians 6:9).

PRACTICAL:

1. What relationship(s) do you need to convert from a debtor's mentality to a prosperity and promise mindset? *(page 74)*

_____

_____

_____

2. Do you believe that debt is a "structural evil" and a hard way to live?

_____ True   _____ False

If you're enslaved by debt, what is your strategy to gain freedom and victory? *(pages 74-75)*

_____

_____

_____

FOR FURTHER STUDY

Get out of debt: *"Owe no man anything, but to love one another: for he that loveth another hath fulfilled the law"* (Romans 13:8); *"Be not entangled again with the yoke of bondage"* (Galatians 5:1; see also James 4:14).

Be on your guard: *"The rich man thinks of his wealth as an impregnable defense, a high wall of safety. What a dreamer!"* (Proverbs 18:11 TLB); *"The attractions of this world and the delights of wealth, and the search for success and lure of nice things come in and crowd out God's message from their hearts, so that no crop is produced"* (Mark 4:19 TLB); *"Be on your guard, lest your hearts be overburdened and depressed (weighed down) with the giddiness and headache and nausea of self-indulgence, drunkenness, and worldly worries and cares pertaining to [the business of] this life, and [lest] that day come upon you suddenly like a trap or a noose"* (Luke 21:34 AMPC).

PRACTICAL:

1. List actions you can take to successfully set your heart on the "three critical Es." *(page 71)*

_____

_____

_____

_____

_____

_____

REPEAT THIS PRAYER OUT LOUD:

Father, in Jesus's name, help me to master the principles that master money. Help me to feed my mind and heart and program my character with truth and encouraging words. I desire to win the debt battle, so I ask for wisdom and strategy. Please guide me by Your Spirit as I sow to the future, and give me grace and mercy as I reap from the past. Amen.

PRINCIPLES I WANT TO MEMORIZE:

SELF-TEST—LESSON 5

1. You do not own what you possess; you are only the steward of it.

   _____ True   _____ False

2. One of the greatest errors we make in stewardship is in our _____. The principle is
   "_____ _____."

3. The use of your money reveals your _____ that come from your
   _____.

4. The number one way to making a profit is: (circle one)

   always using a locally-owned bank.

   serving the customer properly.

   cutting costs with lower quality and higher prices.

5. Financial poverty springs from spiritual poverty in the heart.

   _____ True   _____ False

6. You sow to the _____ and reap from the _____.

7. Good debt management stems from mastering our passions.

   _____ True   _____ False

8. Your life can be summed up in these three words:

   _____, _____, _____

9. Greatness is measured by _____.

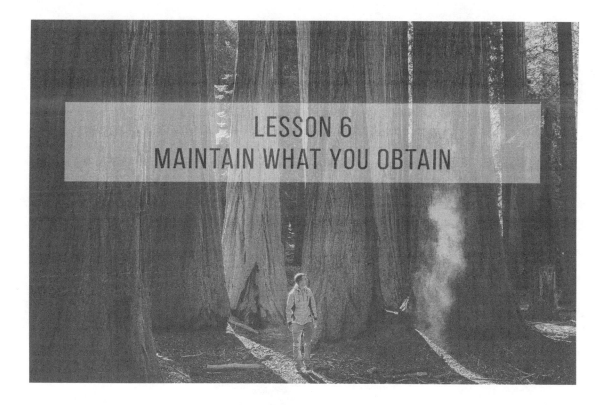

LESSON 6
MAINTAIN WHAT YOU OBTAIN

LESSON 6
MAINTAIN WHAT YOU OBTAIN

A. Fame can come in a moment; greatness comes with _____. *(page 89)*

1. Three major requisites for success are: *(page 89)*

   _____   _____

   _____

2. Counselors determine the destiny of _____. *(page 89)*

3. What is a common weakness in people? *(page 89)*

   _____

4. There is safety in many counselors but be sure to find out: *(page 89–90)*

   what "they" _____
   how "they" _____
   what "they" _____

5. You are never too old to seek counsel. *(page 90)*

   ____ True   ____ False

6. Thinking you know everything is the start of your _____ _____. *(page 90)*

FOR FURTHER STUDY

Mature by a long-term pattern of decisions that enhance your life: *"I have chosen the way of truth: thy judgments have I laid before me"* (Psalm 119:30; see also Romans 5:3–5; 8:37; 2 Timothy 2:21; Hebrews 3:6; 6:1; 1 John 3:2–3).

Counselors determine the destiny of kings (see 2 Samuel 16:23; 1 Kings 14): *"For lack of guidance a nation falls, but victory is won through many advisers make"* (Proverbs 11:14 NIV); *"Better is a poor and wise youth than an old and foolish king who no longer knows how to receive counsel"* (Ecclesiastes 4:13).

Seek God's counsel or you may be deceived. (See Joshua 9:14, 15; Hebrews 11:6.)

Don't be moved by a person's personality, persuasion and belief: *"Stop listening to teaching that contradicts what you know is right"* (Proverbs 19:27 TLB); *"Don't let the world around you squeeze you into its own mould, but let God re-mould your minds from within"* (Romans 12:2 Phillips); *"Be no more children, tossed to and fro...with every wind of doctrine, by the sleight of men"* (Ephesians 4:14).

B. _____ is the basis for relationship. *(page 90)*

1. _____ is the basic art of communication. *(page 91)*

2. You make a success in life by your ability to speak. *(page 91)*

____ True ____ False

3. Prosperity and success are based on what you _____. *(page 91)*

4. Name the three common areas that hinder prospering in a family: *(page 91)*

_____ _____ _____

5. Reliable communication allows for progress. *(page 91)*

____ True ____ False

6. No one ever said on his deathbed that his only regret was not spending more time at the _____. *(page 91)*

C. What is the purpose of leadership? *(circle one)* *(page 93)*

to achieve popularity   to earn a higher salary   to influence   to have a title

1. _____ determine to influence; _____ only happen to. *(page 93)*

2. Build leadership skills upon the foundations of: *(page 93)*

_____ _____ _____

3. We do not influence industries or nations; we only influence _____. *(page 93)*

FOR FURTHER STUDY

Importance of listening: *"The Lord…called…. Samuel answered, Speak; for thy servant heareth"* (1 Samuel 3:10); *"Guard your steps when you go to the house of God. Go near to listen rather than to offer the sacrifice of fools"* (Ecclesiastes 5:1); *"Every idle word that men shall speak, they shall give account thereof in the day of judgment"* (Matthew 12:36).

Rules for communication—with others: *"Let every man be swift to hear, slow to speak, slow to wrath"* (James 1:19); with wives: *"Husbands,… be considerate as you live with your wives, and treat them with respect"* (1 Peter 3:7 NIV); with children: *"Fathers, provoke not your children to wrath: but bring them up in the nurture and admonition of the Lord"* (Ephesians 6:4).

Leadership has the potential for good or harm. (See Proverbs 29:2; 1 Chronicles 28:8–9; Ecclesiastes 10:5). Leadership requires character, integrity and influence. (See Ezra 7:10.)

Leaders must practice what they want others to do: *"Be thou an example of the believers, in word, in conversation, in charity, in spirit, in faith, in purity"* (1 Timothy 4:12; see also 1 Peter 5:3).

---

4. It is wise to use influence but _____ to sell it. *(page 93)*

5. Leaders choose employees to influence who meet one basic criteria, the cornerstone of character: _____. *(page 93)*

6. Three ingredients comprise faithfulness: *(page 93)*

_____ _____ _____

7. Write the correct letter next to the word being defined. *(page 93)*

_____Firmly attached, keeps confidences, stands up for the cause   a. constancy

_____Willingness to subject yourself to another   b. loyalty

_____Never varying, steadfast   c. submission

8. The _____ of the kingdom emanate from the character of the _____. *(page 94)*

9. The basic pattern for management is: *(page 94)*

_____ them   _____ them   _____ them

10. Train employees, give them responsibility, and have them _____ for it, because responsibility without _____ is an error. *(page 94–95)*

11. Sedition is the _____ of constituted _____ with the attempt to _____ it. Sedition is an act of _____, punishable by _____. *(page 95)*

FOR FURTHER STUDY

Faithfulness is the cornerstone of character: *"A faithful man shall abound with blessings"* (Proverbs 28:20; see also Matthew 24:45–47).

Lay a right foundation for your character. (See 2 Corinthians 7:1.)

God commits to character, not talent: *"Well done, thou good and faithful servant: thou hast been faithful over a few things, I will make thee ruler over many things: enter thou into the joy of thy Lord"* (Matthew 25:21; see also Luke 16:10; 2 Timothy 2:2).

Invest in character: *"Moreover it is required in stewards, that a man be found faithful"* (1 Corinthians 4:2; see also Matthew 7:15–16; 2 Peter 1:5–7).

The characteristics of the kingdom emanate from the character of the king: *"'Like priests, like people'—because the priests are wicked, the people are too"* (Hosea 4:9 TLB).

Every man is accountable for six areas of responsibility (based on 1 Timothy 3:1–11): reputation (1 Thessalonians 5:22, 2 Corinthians 6:3); ethics (1 Timothy 4:16); morality and temperament (2 Timothy 2:24–25); habits (1 Timothy 4:8); maturity (1 Timothy 4:15).

D.   What is the essential ingredient in success? *(page 96)*

_____

1. Life management begins with _____ management. *(page 96)*

2. We _____ from the past to _____ in the present what will _____ for the future. *(page 97)*

3. Time is worthy of respect. *(page 97)*

_____ True   _____ False

4. Procrastinators live under _____ stress and at the mercy of those who respect _____. *(page 97)*

5. Organization brings _____. Disorganization brings _____, _____ and _____. *(page 98)*

6. Creativity is stifled when too much time is spent on _____. *(page 98)*

7. Success is based on the ability to say "no." *(page 98)*

_____ True   _____ False

8. Time and money are _____, not goals. But it takes a combination of _____ and _____ to reach our goals. *(page 99)*

FOR FURTHER STUDY

Persevere to mature (see 1 Corinthians 15:58): *"Let us not become weary in doing good, for at the proper time we will reap a harvest if we do not give up"* (Galatians 6:9 NIV; see also 2 Thessalonians 3:13; 1 Timothy 4:16; Hebrews 12:1–3).
God takes us through seasons (Psalm 22:9–11): *"To every thing there is a season, and a time to every purpose under the heaven"* (Ecclesiastes 3:1); *"Listen to me, all Israel who are left; I have created you and cared for you since you were born. I will be your God through all your lifetime, yes, even when your hair is white with age. I made you, and I will care for you. I will carry you along and be your Savior"* (Isaiah 46:3–4 TLB).
Unproductive time: *"He also that is slothful in his work is brother to him that is a great waster"* (Proverbs 18:9); *"By much slothfulness the building decayeth; and through idleness of the hands the house droppeth through"* (Ecclesiastes 10:18).

_____

E. The difference between people who fail and those who succeed often lies in how they handle the
_____ of _____. (*page 99*)

1. Failure is the womb of success. (*page 99*)

_____ True   _____ False

2. What do successful people do with failure? (*check all that apply*) (*page 99*)

_____ write about it in their journal   _____ obsess over it

_____ refuse to live with it   _____ bury it

_____ use it as an excuse for inaction   _____ talk about it

3. "Winners look at what they're going _____; losers look at what they're going
_____." (*page 100*)

4. Overcoming stuff is the difference between those who achieve excellence and those who
_____ in the _____ of _____. (*page 100*)

5. To improve your life, work on: (*circle one*) (*page 100*)

your spouse   your resume   yourself

6. Success is the greatest antidote to failure. (*page 101*)

_____ True   _____ False

FOR FURTHER STUDY

Pressure tests manhood: "You are a poor specimen if you can't stand the pressure of adversity" (Proverbs 24:10 TLB); "*If thou faint in the day of adversity, thy strength is small*" (Proverbs 24:10); "*Blessed is the one who perseveres under trial…having stood the test, that person will receive the crown of life…the Lord has promised to those who love him*" (James 1:12 NIV).

Discipline is the correct application of pressure. (See 1 Corinthians 9:27.)

Successful men handle pressure: "*And David was greatly distressed; for the people spake of stoning him, because the soul of all the people was grieved, every man for his sons and for his daughters: but David encouraged himself in the LORD his God*" (1 Samuel 30:6).

Jesus faced and overcame the ultimate pressure; whoever believes in Him can live in the same way: "*Looking unto Jesus the author and finisher of our faith; who for the joy that was set before him endured the cross, despising the shame, and is set down at the right hand of the throne of God. For consider him that endured such contradiction of sinners against himself, lest ye be wearied and faint in your minds*" (Hebrews 12:2–3; see also Philippians 2:8–9).

7. Maturity does not come with _____ but begins with the _____ of _____. *(page 101)*

8. Responsibility for success is built upon being responsible for failure. *(page 101)*

____ True ____ False

9. Generally, the person who is afraid to fail is also the one who cannot _____ _____. *(page 101)*

10. Failure is not the worst thing in the world—_____ is. *(page 101)*

11. Champions are not those who never _____ but those who never _____. *(page 101)*

F. Build your business before building your own: *(page 101)*

_____ _____ _____

1. Profits are the lifeblood of any economy. *(page 101)*

____ True ____ False

2. Hard _____ brings _____; playing around brings _____. *(page 101)*

3. Above the clouds, the _____ _____ _____. *(page 102)*

FOR FURTHER STUDY

Maturity rests on accepting responsibility: *"He that covereth his sins shall not prosper: but whoso confesseth and forsaketh them shall have mercy"* (Proverbs 28:13; see also Acts 13:22); *"For we must all appear before the judgment seat of Christ; that every one may receive the things done in his body, according to that he hath done, whether it be good or bad"* (2 Corinthians 5:10).

We cannot mature if we blame circumstances or others. (See Proverbs 16:2; 21:2; Genesis 3:11–12.)

Don't quit: *"And let us not be weary in well doing: for in due season we shall reap, if we faint not"* (Galatians 6:9).

Get rich quick schemes: *"Ill-gotten gain brings no lasting happiness; right living does"* (Proverbs 10:2); *"Wealth from hard work grows"* (Proverbs 13:11 TLB); *"Wealth [not earned but] won in haste or unjustly or from the production of things for vain or detrimental use [such riches] will dwindle away, but he who gathers little by little will increase [his riches]"* (Proverbs 13:11 AMPC).

G. Check True or False for the following sentences: *(pages 102–105)*

Relationships precede success. ____ True ____ False

Influence is one of the most precious commodities in life. ____ True ____ False

Personnel is always the problem and always the solution. ____ True ____ False

Organizing time shows respect for time. ____ True ____ False

All success is born out of failure. ____ True ____ False

Every word spoken is worthy to be heard. ____ True ____ False

In front of every promise, there is a problem. ____ True ____ False

H. Write the correct letter next to the word that completes the sentence. *(pages 102–105)*

____ Taking time to listen   a. shows disrespect for self

____ We can't change the seasons   b. are always at their best

____ Only the inferior   c. we can only adapt to them

____ You can commit to character   d. you cannot fail

____ Don't let your workplace   e. shows respect for others

____ Listening to foolish people   f. but what you inspect

____ If we don't communicate   g. become your hiding place

____ Faithfulness is   h. not to talent

____ People don't do what you expect   i. the cornerstone of character

____ If you never quit   j. we can't relate.

FOR FURTHER STUDY

Judge yourself by your actions, not by your intentions: *"A man is known by his actions. An evil man lives an evil life; a good man lives a godly life"* (Proverbs 21:8 AMPC).

Detail God's will and plan for your life. Be a steward of His words by immediate obedience. (See Psalm 119:60; Isaiah 34:16; 1 Timothy 4:14–16.)

Learn from others but seek God to find the individual pattern He has for you alone: *"But you have received the Holy Spirit and he lives within you, in your hearts.... For he teaches you all things, and he is the Truth"* (1 John 2:27 TLB); *"Only a simpleton believes what he is told! A prudent man checks to see where he is going"* (Proverbs 14:15 TLB); *"And he that overcometh, and keepeth my works unto the end, to him will I give power over the nations"* (Revelation 2:26).

PRACTICAL:

1. Time is the great equalizer. *(page 96–97)*

   Explain what this means and how it affects your life.

   _____

   _____

   _____

   _____

2. Resisting the extraneous, illegitimate and unnecessary allows for occupation with the productive, positive and vital. *(page 98)*

   How can you apply this truth?

   _____

   _____

   _____

   _____

REPEAT THIS PRAYER OUT LOUD:

Father, please help me plan wisely, use common sense and be strong in what I know is right. Give me grace and determination to handle adversity. I desire excellence; therefore, I choose to accept responsibility, to work hard, to respect time. Lord, I pray, with Your help, I will stay in 'til I win—to never quit—to prosper. In Jesus's name. Amen.

FOR FURTHER STUDY:

Living your life: *"Be eager and strive earnestly to guard and keep the harmony and oneness of [and produced by] the Spirit in the binding power of peace"* (Ephesians 4:3 AMPC); *"And let the peace…from Christ rule (act as umpire continually) in your hearts"* (Colossians 3:15 AMPC); *"This should be your ambition: to live a quiet life, minding your own business and doing your own work…. As a result, people who are not Christians will trust and respect you, and you will not need to depend on others for enough money to pay your bills"* (1 Thessalonians 4:11–12 TLB).

SELF-TEST—LESSON 6

1. Success is based on the ability to say "no."

    _____ True _____ False

2. Three major requisites for success are:

    _____

    _____

    _____

3. Maturity does not come with _____ but begins with the _____ of _____.

4. You can commit to: (*circle one*)

    talent   personality   character

5. "Winners look at what they're going _____; losers look at what they're going _____."

6. _____ is the basic art of communication.

7. Build leadership skills upon the foundation of

    _____ _____ _____

8. You are never too old to seek counsel.

    _____ True _____ False

9. People don't do what you expect but what you _____.

10. The _____ of the kingdom emanate from the character of the _____.

FINAL EXAM

TREASURE:
UNCOVERING PRINCIPLES THAT GOVERN SUCCESS

1. Evil companionships _____ good character.

2. The loss of the habit of reading is a gain in the realm of _____.

3. Knowing you can do better means you've not done your best.

   _____ True   _____ False

4. Love always desires to benefit _____ at the expense of _____.

5. Lust desires to benefit _____ even at the expense of _____.

6. One of the greatest errors we make in stewardship is in our _____. The principle is
   "_____ _____."

7. Money cannot compensate for the lack of _____ _____.

8. Greatness is measured by _____.

9. You can pitch your _____, but you _____ your
   _____.

10. Every word you speak has creative power.

    ____ True   ____ False

11. Private philosophy determines public performance.

    ____ True   ____ False

12. Humility precedes _____.

13. You sow to the _____ and reap from the _____.

14. "Winners look at what they're going _____; losers look at what they're going _____."

15. Learning requires a heart for _____ and a desire to be _____.

16. Images in our minds drive us toward our _____.

17. Gifts and talents are never earned, only discovered.

    ____ True   ____ False

18. You can commit to: *(circle one)*

    talent   personality   character

19. The use of your money reveals your _____ that come from your _____.

20. The issues of life spring from your heart.

    _____ True   _____ False

21. The most powerful thing you can do in life is _____. *(circle one)*

    own a business   create an image   run for office   win the lottery

22. True humility is simply the willingness to _____.

23. People and nations are not great by _____ of their _____ but by the _____ of their _____.

24. The number one way to making a profit is: *(circle one)*

    always using a locally owned bank.

    serving the customer properly.

    cutting costs with lower quality and higher prices.

25. Build leadership skills upon the foundation of

    _____   _____   _____

26. You do not own what you possess; you are only the steward of it.

    _____ True   _____ False

27. It is possible for your talent to take you to a place where your _____ cannot _____ you.

28. Good debt management stems from mastering our passions.

    ____ True   ____ False

29. Maturity does not come with _____ but begins with the _____ of _____.

30. Trust is extended to the limit of truth and no more.

    ____ True   ____ False

31. True wealth comes from your _____.

32. It is always easier to _____ than to _____.

33. Choices determine what three things:

    _____   _____   _____

34. Good is the _____ of best.

35. _____ is the basic art of communication.

36. Success is based on the ability to say "no."

      ____ True   ____ False

37. Once you make a choice, you become the _____ to that choice.

38. All of life depends on relationships.

      ____ True   ____ False

39. People don't do what you expect but what you _____.

40. What you think in your heart determines what you _____. *(circle one)*

      have for lunch   do on vacation   become

41. Life is composed of your choices and constructed by your words.

      ____ True   ____ False

42. Faith is _____ in action. *(circle one)*

      discovery   experience   enthusiasm   belief

43. Wealth will get you riches, but they will never make you _____.

44. Strongly held opinions will hold up to truth.

      ____ True   ____ False

45. Short essay: "Everything in life follows a pattern, based on a principle."

Analyze that statement, giving examples of real-life situations where it has proven to be true. How does it apply to your daily life?

_____

_____

_____

_____

_____

_____

_____

_____

_____

_____

_____

_____

_____

_____

_____

_____

_____

_____

_____

_____

_____

_____

_____

_____

_____

_____

_____

Name _____

Address _____

City _____ State _____ Zip_____

Telephone: a.m. _____ p.m. _____

Email address: _____

The Final Exam is required to be "commissioned."

For more information, contact

Christian Men's Network / P.O. Box 3 / Grapevine, TX 76099

www.ChristianMensNetwork.com / office@ChristianMensNetwork.com / 817-437-4888

Basic Daily Bible Reading

Read Proverbs each morning for wisdom, Psalms each evening for courage. Make copies of this chart and keep it in your Bible to mark o you read. If you are just starting the habit of Bible reading, be aware that longer translations or paraphrases (such as Amplified and Living) take longer to read each day. As you start, it is okay to read only one of the chapters in Psalms each night, instead of the many listed. Mark chart so you'll remember which ones you haven't read.

NOTE: The chronological chart following has the rest of the chapters of Psalms that are not listed here. By using both charts together, you cover the entire book of Psalms.

Day of Month	Proverbs	Psalms	Day of Month	Proverbs	Psalms
1	1	1, 2, 4, 5, 6			
2	2	7, 8, 9	18	18	82, 83, 84, 85
3	3	10, 11, 12, 13, 14, 15	19	19	87, 88, 91, 92
4	4	16, 17, 19, 20	20	20	93, 94, 95, 97
5	5	21, 22, 23	21	21	98, 99, 100, 101, 103
6	6	24, 25, 26, 27	22	22	104, 108
7	7	28, 29, 31, 32	23	23	109, 110, 111
8	8	33, 35	24	24	112, 113, 114, 115, 117
9	9	36, 37	25	25	119:1-56
10	10	38, 39, 40	26	26	119:57-112
11	11	41, 42, 43, 45, 46	27	27	119:113-176
12	12	47, 48, 49, 50	28	28	120, 121, 122, 124, 130
13	13	53, 55, 58, 61, 62			131, 133, 134
14	14	64, 65, 66, 67	29	29	135, 136, 138
15	15	68, 69	30	30	139, 140, 141, 143
16	16	70, 71, 73	31	31	144, 145, 146, 148, 150
17	17	75, 76, 77, 81			

Chronological Annual Bible Reading

This schedule follows the events of the Bible chronologically and can be used with any translation or paraphrase of the Bible. Each day ha average of 77 verses of Scripture. If you follow this annually, along with your Daily Bible Reading, by your third year, you will recognize where are and what is going to happen next. By your fifth year, you will understand the Scriptural background and setting for any reference spoken a message or book. At that point, the Word will become more like "meat" to you and less like "milk." Once you understand the basic stories what happens on the surface, God can reveal to you the layers of meaning beneath. So, make copies of this chart to keep in your Bible and r off as you read. And start reading—it's the greatest adventure in life!

Some notes:
1. Some modern translations don't have verses numbered (such as The Message), so they cannot be used with this chart. Also, if you are starting the Bible, be aware that longer translations or paraphrases (such as Amplified and Living) tend to take longer to read each day.
2. The Daily Bible Reading chart covers the Proverbs and the chapters of Psalms that are not listed here. By using both charts together, you cover the entire books of Psalms and Proverbs along with the rest of the Bible.
3. The chronology of Scripture is obvious in some cases, educated guesswork in others. The placement of Job, for example, is purely conje since there is no consensus among Bible scholars as to its date or place. For the most part, however, chronological reading helps the reader, it places stories that have duplicated information, or prophetic utterances elsewhere in Scripture, within the same reading sequence.

HOW TO READ SCRIPTURE NOTATIONS:
Book chapter: verse. (Mark 15:44 means the book of Mark, chapter 15, verse 44.)
Book chapter; chapter (Mark 15; 16; 17 means the book of Mark, chapters 15, 16, 17.)
Books continue the same until otherwise noted. (2 Kings 22; 23:1-28; Jeremiah 20 means the book of 2 Kings, chapter 22, the book of 2 Kings, chapter 23, verses 1-28; then the book of Jeremiah, chapter 20.)

MAJORING IN MEN®

1	Jan 1	Genesis 1; 2; 3
2	Jan 2	Genesis 4; 5; 6
3	Jan 3	Genesis 7; 8; 9
4	Jan 4	Genesis 10; 11; 12
5	Jan 5	Genesis 13; 14; 15; 16
6	Jan 6	Genesis 17; 18; 19:1-29
7	Jan 7	Genesis 19:30-38; 20; 21
8	Jan 8	Genesis 22; 23; 24:1-31
9	Jan 9	Genesis 24:32-67; 25
10	Jan 10	Genesis 26; 27
11	Jan 11	Genesis 28; 29; 30:1-24
12	Jan 12	Genesis 30:25-43; 31
13	Jan 13	Genesis 32; 33; 34
14	Jan 14	Genesis 35; 36
15	Jan 15	Genesis 37; 38; 39
16	Jan 16	Genesis 40; 41
17	Jan 17	Genesis 42; 43
18	Jan 18	Genesis 44; 45
19	Jan 19	Genesis 46; 47; 48
20	Jan 20	Genesis 49; 50; Exodus 1
21	Jan 21	Exodus 2; 3; 4
22	Jan 22	Exodus 5; 6; 7
23	Jan 23	Exodus 8; 9
24	Jan 24	Exodus 10; 11; 12
25	Jan 25	Exodus 13; 14; 15
26	Jan 26	Exodus 16; 17; 18
27	Jan 27	Exodus 19; 20; 21
28	Jan 28	Exodus 22; 23; 24
29	Jan 29	Exodus 25; 26
30	Jan 30	Exodus 27; 28; 29:1-28
31	Jan 31	Exodus 29:29-46; 30; 31
32	Feb 1	Exodus 32; 33; 34
33	Feb 2	Exodus 35; 36
34	Feb 3	Exodus 37; 38
35	Feb 4	Exodus 39; 40
36	Feb 5	Leviticus 1; 2; 3; 4
37	Feb 6	Leviticus 5; 6; 7
38	Feb 7	Leviticus 8; 9; 10
39	Feb 8	Leviticus 11; 12; 13:1-37
40	Feb 9	Leviticus 13:38-59; 14
41	Feb 10	Leviticus 15; 16
42	Feb 11	Leviticus 17; 18; 19
43	Feb 12	Leviticus 20; 21; 22:1-16
44	Feb 13	Leviticus 22:17-33; 23
45	Feb 14	Leviticus 24; 25
46	Feb 15	Leviticus 26; 27
47	Feb 16	Numbers 1; 2
48	Feb 17	Numbers 3; 4:1-20
49	Feb 18	Numbers 4:21-49; 5; 6
50	Feb 19	Numbers 7
51	Feb 20	Numbers 8; 9; 10
52	Feb 21	Numbers 11; 12; 13
53	Feb 22	Numbers 14; 15
54	Feb 23	Numbers 16; 17
55	Feb 24	Numbers 18; 19; 20
56	Feb 25	Numbers 21; 22
57	Feb 26	Numbers 23; 24; 25
58	Feb 27	Numbers 26; 27
59	Feb 28	Numbers 28; 29; 30
60	Mar 1	Numbers 31; 32:1-27
61	Mar 2	Numbers 32:28-42; 33

62	Mar 3	Numbers 34; 35; 36
63	Mar 4	Deuteronomy 1; 2
64	Mar 5	Deuteronomy 3; 4
65	Mar 6	Deuteronomy 5; 6; 7
66	Mar 7	Deuteronomy 8; 9; 10
67	Mar 8	Deuteronomy 11; 12; 13
68	Mar 9	Deuteronomy 14; 15; 16
69	Mar 10	Deuteronomy 17; 18; 19; 20
70	Mar 11	Deuteronomy 21; 22; 23
71	Mar 12	Deuteronomy 24; 25; 26; 27
72	Mar 13	Deuteronomy 28
73	Mar 14	Deuteronomy 29; 30; 31
74	Mar 15	Deuteronomy 32; 33
75	Mar 16	Deuteronomy 34; Psalm 90; Joshua 1; 2
76	Mar 17	Joshua 3; 4; 5; 6
77	Mar 18	Joshua 7; 8; 9
78	Mar 19	Joshua 10; 11
79	Mar 20	Joshua 12; 13; 14
80	Mar 21	Joshua 15; 16
81	Mar 22	Joshua 17; 18; 19:1-23
82	Mar 23	Joshua 19:24-51; 20; 21
83	Mar 24	Joshua 22; 23; 24
84	Mar 25	Judges 1; 2; 3:1-11
85	Mar 26	Judges 3:12-31; 4; 5
86	Mar 27	Judges 6; 7
87	Mar 28	Judges 8; 9
88	Mar 29	Judges 10; 11; 12
89	Mar 30	Judges 13; 14; 15
90	Mar 31	Judges 16; 17; 18
91	Apr 1	Judges 19; 20
		[You have completed 1/4 of the Bible!]
92	Apr 2	Judges 21; Job 1; 2; 3
93	Apr 3	Job 4; 5; 6
94	Apr 4	Job 7; 8; 9
95	Apr 5	Job 10; 11; 12
96	Apr 6	Job 13; 14; 15
97	Apr 7	Job 16; 17; 18; 19
98	Apr 8	Job 20; 21
99	Apr 9	Job 22; 23; 24
100	Apr 10	Job 25; 26; 27; 28
101	Apr 11	Job 29; 30; 31
102	Apr 12	Job 32; 33; 34
103	Apr 13	Job 35; 36; 37
104	Apr 14	Job 38; 39
105	Apr 15	Job 40; 41; 42
106	Apr 16	Ruth 1; 2; 3
107	Apr 17	Ruth 4; 1 Samuel 1; 2
108	Apr 18	1 Samuel 3; 4; 5; 6
109	Apr 19	1 Samuel 7; 8; 9
110	Apr 20	1 Samuel 10; 11; 12; 13
111	Apr 21	1 Samuel 14; 15
112	Apr 22	1 Samuel 16; 17
113	Apr 23	1 Samuel 18; 19; Psalm 59
114	Apr 24	1 Samuel 20; 21; Psalms 34; 56
115	Apr 25	1 Samuel 22; 23, Psalms 52; 142
116	Apr 26	1 Samuel 24; 25; 1 Chronicles 12:8-18; Psalm 57
117	Apr 27	1 Samuel 26; 27; 28; Psalms 54; 63
118	Apr 28	1 Samuel 29; 30; 31; 1 Chronicles 12:1-7; 12:19-22

119	Apr 29	1 Chronicles 10; 2 Samuel 1; 2
120	Apr 30	2 Samuel 3; 4; 1 Chronicles 11:1-9; 12:23-40
121	May 1	2 Samuel 5; 6; 1 Chronicles 13; 14
122	May 2	2 Samuel 22; 1 Chronicles 15
123	May 3	1 Chronicles 16; Psalm 18
124	May 4	2 Samuel 7; Psalms 96; 105
125	May 5	1 Chronicles 17; 2 Samuel 8; 9; 10
126	May 6	1 Chronicles 18; 19; Psalm 60; 2 Samuel 11
127	May 7	2 Samuel 12; 13; 1 Chronicles 20:1-3; Psalm 51
128	May 8	2 Samuel 14; 15
129	May 9	2 Samuel 16; 17; 18; Psalm 3
130	May 10	2 Samuel 19; 20; 21
131	May 11	2 Samuel 23:8-23
132	May 12	1 Chronicles 20:4-8; 11:10-25; 2 Samuel 23:24-39; 24
133	May 13	1 Chronicles 11:26-47; 21; 22
134	May 14	1 Chronicles 23; 24; Psalm 30
135	May 15	1 Chronicles 25; 26
136	May 16	1 Chronicles 27; 28; 29
137	May 17	1 Kings 1; 2:1-12; 2 Samuel 23:1-7
138	May 18	1 Kings 2:13-46; 3; 2 Chronicles 1:1-13
139	May 19	1 Kings 5; 6; 2 Chronicles 2
140	May 20	1 Kings 7; 2 Chronicles 3; 4
141	May 21	1 Kings 8; 2 Chronicles 5
142	May 22	1 Kings 9; 2 Chronicles 6; 7:1-10
143	May 23	1 Kings 10:1-13; 2 Chronicles 7:11-22; 8; 9:1-12; 1 Kings 4
144	May 24	1 Kings 10:14-29; 2 Chronicles 1:14-17; 9:13-28; Psalms 72; 127
145	May 25	Song of Solomon 1; 2; 3; 4; 5
146	May 26	Song of Solomon 6; 7; 8; 1 Kings 11:1-40
147	May 27	Ecclesiastes 1; 2; 3; 4
148	May 28	Ecclesiastes 5; 6; 7; 8
149	May 29	Ecclesiastes 9; 10; 11; 12; 1 Kings 11:41-43; 2 Chronicles 9:29-31
150	May 30	1 Kings 12; 2 Chronicles 10; 11
151	May 31	1 Kings 13; 14; 2 Chronicles 12
152	June 1	1 Kings 15; 2 Chronicles 13; 14; 15
153	June 2	1 Kings 16; 2 Chronicles 16; 17
154	June 3	1 Kings 17; 18; 19
155	June 4	1 Kings 20; 21
156	June 5	1 Kings 22; 2 Chronicles 18
157	June 6	2 Chronicles 19; 20; 2 Kings 1; 3
158	June 7	2 Kings 2; 4; 6
159	June 8	2 Kings 5; 8; 2 Chronicles 21
160	June 9	2 Kings 7; 9; 2 Chronicles 22
161	June 10	2 Kings 10; 11; 2 Chronicles 23
162	June 11	Joel 1; 2; 3
163	June 12	2 Kings 12; 13; 2 Chronicles 24
164	June 13	2 Kings 14; 2 Chronicles 25; Jonah 1
165	June 14	Jonah 2; 3; 4; Hosea 1; 2; 3; 4
166	June 15	Hosea 5; 6; 7; 8; 9; 10
167	June 16	Hosea 11; 12; 13; 14

168	June 17	2 Kings 15:1-7;
		2 Chronicles 26; Amos 1; 2; 3
169	June 18	Amos 4; 5; 6; 7
170	June 19	Amos 8; 9; 2 Kings 15:8-18;
		Isaiah 1
171	June 20	Isaiah 2; 3; 4; 2 Kings 15:19-38;
		2 Chronicles 27
172	June 21	Isaiah 5; 6; Micah 1; 2; 3
173	June 22	Micah 4; 5; 6; 7; 2 Kings 16:1-18
174	June 23	2 Chronicles 28; Isaiah 7; 8
175	June 24	Isaiah 9; 10; 11; 12
176	June 25	Isaiah 13; 14; 15; 16
177	June 26	Isaiah 17; 18; 19; 20; 21
178	June 27	Isaiah 22; 23; 24; 25
179	June 28	Isaiah 26; 27; 28; 29
180	June 29	Isaiah 30; 31; 32; 33
181	June 30	Isaiah 34, 35, 2 Kings 16:19-20;
		18:1-8; 2 Chronicles 29
182	July 1	2 Chronicles 30; 31; 2 Kings 17
		[You have completed 1/2 of the Bible!]
183	July 2	2 Kings 18:9-37;
		2 Chronicles 32:1-19; Isaiah 36
184	July 3	2 Kings 19; 2 Chronicles 32:20-23;
		Isaiah 37
185	July 4	2 Kings 20; 21:1-18; 2 Chronicles
		32:24-33; Isaiah 38; 39
186	July 5	2 Chronicles 33:1-20; Isaiah 40; 41
187	July 6	Isaiah 42; 43; 44
188	July 7	Isaiah 45; 46; 47; 48
189	July 8	Isaiah 49; 50; 51; 52
190	July 9	Isaiah 53; 54; 55; 56; 57
191	July 10	Isaiah 58; 59; 60; 61; 62
192	July 11	Isaiah 63; 64; 65; 66
193	July 12	2 Kings 21:19-26; 2 Chronicles
		33:21-25; 34:1-7; Zephaniah 1; 2; 3
194	July 13	Jeremiah 1; 2; 3
195	July 14	Jeremiah 4; 5
196	July 15	Jeremiah 6; 7; 8
197	July 16	Jeremiah 9; 10; 11
198	July 17	Jeremiah 12; 13; 14; 15
199	July 18	Jeremiah 16; 17; 18; 19
200	July 19	Jeremiah 20; 2 Kings 22; 23:1-28
201	July 20	2 Chronicles 34:8-33; 35:1-19;
		Nahum 1; 2; 3
202	July 21	2 Kings 23:29-37; 2 Chronicles
		35:20-27; 36:1-5; Jeremiah
		22:10-17; 26; Habakkuk 1
203	July 22	Habakkuk 2; 3; Jeremiah 46; 47;
		2 Kings 24:1-4; 2 Chronicles 36:6-7
204	July 23	Jeremiah 25; 35; 36; 45
205	July 24	Jeremiah 48; 49:1-33
206	July 25	Daniel 1; 2
207	July 26	Jeremiah 22:18-30; 2 Kings
		24:5-20; 2 Chronicles 36:8-12;
		Jeremiah 37:1-2; 52:1-3; 24; 29
208	July 27	Jeremiah 27; 28; 23
209	July 28	Jeremiah 50; 51:1-19
210	July 29	Jeremiah 51:20-64; 49:34-39; 34
211	July 30	Ezekiel 1; 2; 3; 4
212	July 31	Ezekiel 5; 6; 7; 8

213	Aug 1	Ezekiel 9; 10; 11; 12
214	Aug 2	Ezekiel 13, 14, 15, 16:1-34
215	Aug 3	Ezekiel 16:35-63; 17; 18
216	Aug 4	Ezekiel 19; 20
217	Aug 5	Ezekiel 21; 22
218	Aug 6	Ezekiel 23; 2 Kings 25:1;
		2 Chronicles 36:13-16;
		Jeremiah 39:1; 52:4; Ezekiel 24
219	Aug 7	Jeremiah 21; 22:1-9; 32; 30
220	Aug 8	Jeremiah 31; 33; Ezekiel 25
221	Aug 9	Ezekiel 29:1-16; 30; 31; 26
222	Aug 10	Ezekiel 27; 28; Jeremiah 37:3-21
223	Aug 11	Jeremiah 38; 39:2-10; 52:5-30
224	Aug 12	2 Kings 25:2-22; 2 Chronicles
		36:17-21; Jeremiah 39:11-18;
		40:1-6; Lamentations 1
225	Aug 13	Lamentations 2; 3
226	Aug 14	Lamentations 4; 5; Obadiah;
		Jeremiah 40:7-16
227	Aug 15	Jeremiah 41; 42; 43; 44;
		2 Kings 25:23-26
228	Aug 16	Ezekiel 33:21-33; 34; 35; 36
229	Aug 17	Ezekiel 37; 38; 39
230	Aug 18	Ezekiel 32; 33:1-20; Daniel 3
231	Aug 19	Ezekiel 40; 41
232	Aug 20	Ezekiel 42; 43; 44
233	Aug 21	Ezekiel 45; 46; 47
234	Aug 22	Ezekiel 48; 29:17-21; Daniel 4
235	Aug 23	Jeremiah 52:31-34; 2 Kings
		25:27-30; Psalms 44; 74; 79
236	Aug 24	Psalms 80; 86; 89
237	Aug 25	Psalms 102; 106
238	Aug 26	Psalms 123; 137; Daniel 7; 8
239	Aug 27	Daniel 5; 9; 6
240	Aug 28	2 Chronicles 36:22-23; Ezra 1; 2
241	Aug 29	Ezra 3; 4:1-5; Daniel 10; 11
242	Aug 30	Daniel 12; Ezra 4:6-24; 5;
		6:1-13; Haggai 1
243	Aug 31	Haggai 2; Zechariah 1; 2; 3
244	Sept 1	Zechariah 4; 5; 6; 7; 8
245	Sept 2	Ezra 6:14-22; Psalm 78
246	Sept 3	Psalms 107; 116; 118
247	Sept 4	Psalms 125; 126; 128; 129;
		132; 147
248	Sept 5	Psalm 149; Zechariah 9; 10;
		11; 12; 13
249	Sept 6	Zechariah 14; Esther 1; 2; 3
250	Sept 7	Esther 4; 5; 6; 7; 8
251	Sept 8	Esther 9; 10; Ezra 7; 8
252	Sept 9	Ezra 9; 10; Nehemiah 1
253	Sept 10	Nehemiah 2; 3; 4; 5
254	Sept 11	Nehemiah 6; 7
255	Sept 12	Nehemiah 8; 9; 10
256	Sept 13	Nehemiah 11; 12
257	Sept 14	Nehemiah 13; Malachi 1; 2; 3; 4
258	Sept 15	1 Chronicles 1; 2:1-35
259	Sept 16	1 Chronicles 2:36-55; 3; 4
260	Sept 17	1 Chronicles 5; 6:1-41
261	Sept 18	1 Chronicles 6:42-81; 7
262	Sept 19	1 Chronicles 8; 9
263	Sept 20	Matthew 1; 2; 3; 4

264	Sept 21	Matthew 5; 6
265	Sept 22	Matthew 7; 8
266	Sept 23	Matthew 9; 10
267	Sept 24	Matthew 11; 12
268	Sept 25	Matthew 13; 14
269	Sept 26	Matthew 15; 16
270	Sept 27	Matthew 17; 18; 19
271	Sept 28	Matthew 20; 21
272	Sept 29	Matthew 22; 23
273	Sept 30	Matthew 24; 25
		[You have completed 3/4 of the Bible!]
274	Oct 1	Matthew 26; 27; 28
275	Oct 2	Mark 1; 2
276	Oct 3	Mark 3; 4
277	Oct 4	Mark 5; 6
278	Oct 5	Mark 7; 8:1-26
279	Oct 6	Mark 8:27-38; 9
280	Oct 7	Mark 10; 11
281	Oct 8	Mark 12; 13
282	Oct 9	Mark 14
283	Oct 10	Mark 15; 16
284	Oct 11	Luke 1
285	Oct 12	Luke 2; 3
286	Oct 13	Luke 4; 5
287	Oct 14	Luke 6; 7:1-23
288	Oct 15	Luke 7:24-50; 8
289	Oct 16	Luke 9
290	Oct 17	Luke 10; 11
291	Oct 18	Luke 12; 13
292	Oct 19	Luke 14; 15
293	Oct 20	Luke 16; 17
294	Oct 21	Luke 18; 19
295	Oct 22	Luke 20; 21
296	Oct 23	Luke 22
297	Oct 24	Luke 23; 24:1-28
298	Oct 25	Luke 24:29-53; John 1
299	Oct 26	John 2; 3; 4:1-26
300	Oct 27	John 4:27-54; 5; 6:1-7
301	Oct 28	John 6:8-71; 7:1-21
302	Oct 29	John 7:22-53; 8
303	Oct 30	John 9; 10
304	Oct 31	John 11; 12:1-28
305	Nov 1	John 12:29-50; 13; 14
306	Nov 2	John 15; 16; 17
307	Nov 3	John 18; 19:1-24
308	Nov 4	John 19:25-42; 20; 21
309	Nov 5	Acts 1; 2
310	Nov 6	Acts 3; 4
311	Nov 7	Acts 5; 6
312	Nov 8	Acts 7
313	Nov 9	Acts 8; 9
314	Nov 10	Acts 10
315	Nov 11	Acts 11
316	Nov 12	Acts 12; 13
317	Nov 13	Acts 14; 15; Galatians 1
318	Nov 14	Galatians 2; 3; 4
319	Nov 15	Galatians 5; 6; James 1
320	Nov 16	James 2; 3; 4; 5
321	Nov 17	Acts 16; 17
322	Nov 18	Acts 18:1-11;
		1 Thessalonians 1; 2; 3; 4

DETACH HERE

323	Nov 19	1 Thessalonians 5;
		2 Thessalonians 1; 2; 3
324	Nov 20	Acts 18:12-28; 19:1-22;
		1 Corinthians 1
325	Nov 21	1 Corinthians 2; 3; 4; 5
326	Nov 22	1 Corinthians 6; 7; 8
327	Nov 23	1 Corinthians 9; 10; 11
328	Nov 24	1 Corinthians 12; 13; 14
329	Nov 25	1 Corinthians 15; 16
330	Nov 26	Acts 19:23-41; 20:1;
		2 Corinthians 1; 2
331	Nov 27	2 Corinthians 3; 4; 5
332	Nov 28	2 Corinthians 6; 7; 8; 9
333	Nov 29	2 Corinthians 10; 11; 12
334	Nov 30	2 Corinthians 13; Romans 1; 2
335	Dec 1	Romans 3; 4; 5
336	Dec 2	Romans 6; 7; 8
337	Dec 3	Romans 9; 10; 11

338	Dec 4	Romans 12; 13; 14
339	Dec 5	Romans 15; 16
340	Dec 6	Acts 20:2-38; 21
341	Dec 7	Acts 22; 23
342	Dec 8	Acts 24; 25; 26
343	Dec 9	Acts 27; 28
344	Dec 10	Ephesians 1; 2; 3
345	Dec 11	Ephesians 4; 5; 6
346	Dec 12	Colossians 1; 2; 3
347	Dec 13	Colossians 4; Philippians 1; 2
348	Dec 14	Philippians 3; 4; Philemon
349	Dec 15	1 Timothy 1; 2; 3; 4
350	Dec 16	1 Timothy 5; 6; Titus 1; 2
351	Dec 17	Titus 3; 2 Timothy 1; 2; 3
352	Dec 18	2 Timothy 4; 1 Peter 1; 2
353	Dec 19	1 Peter 3; 4; 5; Jude
354	Dec 20	2 Peter 1; 2; 3; Hebrews 1
355	Dec 21	Hebrews 2; 3; 4; 5

356	Dec 22	Hebrews 6; 7; 8; 9
357	Dec 23	Hebrews 10; 11
358	Dec 24	Hebrews 12; 13; 2 John; 3 John
359	Dec 25	1 John 1; 2; 3; 4
360	Dec 26	1 John 5; Revelation 1; 2
361	Dec 27	Revelation 3; 4; 5; 6
362	Dec 28	Revelation 7; 8; 9; 10; 11
363	Dec 29	Revelation 12; 13; 14; 15
364	Dec 30	Revelation 16; 17; 18; 19
365	Dec 31	Revelation 20; 21; 22

You have completed the entire Bible-Congratulations!

MANHOOD GROWTH PLAN

Order the corresponding workbook for each book, and study the first four Majoring In Men® Curriculum books in this order:

MAXIMIZED MANHOOD: Realize your need for God in every area of your life and start mending relationships with Christ and your family.

COURAGE: Make peace with your past, learn the power of forgiveness and the value of character. Let yourself be challenged to speak up for Christ to other men.

COMMUNICATION, SEX AND MONEY: Increase your ability to communicate, place the right values on sex and money in relationships, and greatly improve relationships, whether married or single.

STRONG MEN IN TOUGH TIMES: Reframe trials, battles and discouragement in light of Scripture and gain solid footing for business, career, and relational choices in the future.

Choose five of the following books to study next. When you have completed nine books, if you are not in men's group, you can find a Majoring In Men® group near you and become "commissioned" to minister to other men.

DARING: Overcome fear to live a life of daring ambition for Godly pursuits.

SEXUAL INTEGRITY: Recognize the sacredness of the sexual union, overcome mistakes and blunders and commit to righteousness in your sexuality.

UNIQUE WOMAN: Discover what makes a woman tick, from adolescence through maturity, to be able to minister to a spouse's uniqueness at any age.

NEVER QUIT: Take the ten steps for entering or leaving any situation, job, relationship or crisis in life.

REAL MAN: Discover the deepest meaning of Christlikeness and learn to exercise good character in times of stress, success or failure.

POWER OF POTENTIAL: Start making solid business and career choices based on Biblical principles while building core character that affects your entire life.

ABSOLUTE ANSWERS: Adopt practical habits and pursue Biblical solutions to overcome "prodigal problems" and secret sins that hinder both success and satisfaction with life.

TREASURE: Practice Biblical solutions and principles on the job to find treasures such as the satisfaction of exercising integrity and a job well done.

IRRESISTIBLE HUSBAND: Avoid common mistakes that sabotage a relationship and learn simple solutions and good habits to build a marriage that will consistently increase in intensity for decades.

CHURCH GROWTH PLAN
STRONG - SUSTAINABLE - SYNERGISTIC
THREE PRACTICAL PHASES TO A POWERFUL MEN'S MOVEMENT IN YOUR CHURCH

Phase One:
- Pastor disciples key men/men's director using Maximized Manhood system.
- Launch creates momentum among men
- Church becomes more attractive to hold men who visit
- Families grow stronger
- Men increase bond to pastor

Phase Two:
- Men/men's director teach other men within the church
- Increased tithing and giving by men
- Decreased number of families in crisis
- Increased mentoring of teens and children
- Increase of male volunteers
- Faster assimilation for men visitors - clear path for pastor to connect with new men
- Men pray regularly for pastor

Phase Three:
- Men teach other men outside the church and bring them to Christ
- Increased male population and attraction to a visiting man, seeing a place he belongs
- Stronger, better-attended community outreaches
- Men are loyal to and support pastor

This system enables the pastor to successfully train key leaders, create momentum, build a church that attracts and holds men who visit, and disciple strong men.

Churches may conduct men's ministry entirely free of charge! Learn how by calling 817-437-4888.

ABOUT THE AUTHOR

Edwin Louis Cole mentored hundreds of thousands of people through challenging events and powerful books that have become the most widely-used Christian men's resources in the world. He is known for pithy statements and a confrontational style that demanded social responsibility and family leadership.

After serving as a pastor, evangelist, and Christian television pioneer, and at an age when most men were retiring, he followed his greatest passion-to lead men into Christlikeness, which he called "real manhood."

Ed Cole was a real man through and through. A loving son to earthly parents and the heavenly Father. Devoted husband to the "loveliest lady in the land," Nancy Corbett Cole. Dedicated father to three and, over the years, accepting the role of "father" to thousands. A reader, a thinker, a visionary. A man who made mistakes, learned lessons, then shared the wealth of his wisdom with men around the world. The Christian Men's Network he founded in 1977 is still a vibrant, global ministry. Unquestionably, he was the greatest men's minister of his generation.